William & Catherine's New Royal Family

Celebrating the arrival of Princess Charlotte

THIS IS A CARLTON BOOK

Published in 2015 by Carlton Books Limited
20 Mortimer Street
London W1T 3JW

10 9 8 7 6 5 4 3 2 1

Text © Carlton Books Ltd 2015
Design © Carlton Books Ltd 2015

A CIP catalogue record for this book is available from the British Library.

ISBN 978 1 78097 662 4

Printed in Spain

William & Catherine's New Royal Family

Celebrating the arrival of Princess Charlotte

IAN LLOYD

CARLTON
BOOKS

CONTENTS

INTRODUCTION

William and Catherine always made it clear they wanted more than one child, particularly as they are both close to their own siblings.

There is more or less the same age gap between William and his younger brother Harry and between Kate and her sister Pippa as there is between Prince George and his sister. Harry has been not just William's brother but also his closest friend. The younger, more outgoing and confident prince has helped the future king to come to terms with his very public role in life.

The untimely death of their mother in 1997 brought the two brothers closer than ever. Only they know what life is like growing up in the royal goldfish bowl, surrounded 24 hours a day by security guards and under the constant scrutiny of the press and public.

Similarly a close family bond unites Kate with Pippa, their brother James and parents Michael and Carole. Early in 2015 the family holidayed together in Mustique to celebrate Carole's 60th birthday, having just a few weeks earlier enjoyed Christmas together at the Cambridges' home in Norfolk, Anmer Hall.

For a future King and Queen a second child is also a dynastic requirement. Princess Diana jokingly called Harry "the spare" to William's heir. The last only child to succeed to the British throne was Queen Victoria, born in 1819.

Both the present Queen's father and grandfather were second sons. George VI's elder brother Edward VIII abdicated in 1936 to marry an American socialite, Wallis Simpson. George V's elder brother, the Duke of Clarence, died from influenza that developed into pneumonia in 1892.

Barring such an eventuality, there is no other constitutional role for a second child. The Queen's sister Princess Margaret, a great beauty with a sharp mind, never found a fulfilling role, other than to support Elizabeth. By the age of 18, she was no longer even the "spare", that role being assumed by the newly born Prince Charles. A generation later, Prince Andrew, was his "spare". An excellent pilot, he served with the Royal Navy during the Falklands War – and just one week after the end of hostilities, William was born and the young naval officer lost his constitutional role.

More recently, and only until the birth of George, Prince Harry, was a "spare" who managed to overcome negative press coverage of his private life by frontline service in Afghanistan and his work with injured ex-service personnel.

His role within the royal family remains important. Indeed his father, Charles, has said that when he eventually becomes king, he wants to slim down the monarchy so that only his two sons and their children are the focus of the institution.

The Cambridges' second child will therefore not only be an ally and supporter to Prince George, but will also play a significant role in the future of the British monarchy.

LEFT: *The Duke and Duchess of Cambridge emerge from hospital carrying Her Royal Highness Princess Charlotte of Cambridge on 2 May 2015.*

A ROYAL TIMELINE

9 January 1982
Catherine Elizabeth Middleton is born at the Royal Berkshire Hospital, Reading.

21 June 1982
William Arthur Philip Louis is born at St Mary's Hospital, Paddington, London.

September 1995
William starts at Eton College, where he gains nine GCSEs and three A-levels.

April 1996
Catherine starts at Marlborough College, where she gains 11 GCSEs and three A-levels.

23 September 2001
William and Catherine start degree courses at St Andrews University.

March 2002
Catherine makes an impression on William at a charity fashion show.

September 2002
Along with two friends, Catherine and William move into a shared flat.

End of 2002, beginning of 2003
Catherine and William become a couple, and try to keep it secret.

September 2004
The couple move to Balgove House on the Strathtyrum estate.

April 2004
William and Catherine go skiing in Klosters and their romance becomes public knowledge.

23 June 2005
Catherine graduates with a 2.1 in Art History and William gets a 2.1 in Geography.

January 2006
William begins army training at Sandhurst, and with romance virtually "on hold" Catherine is dubbed "Waity Katie" by the press.

March 2006
Catherine makes her first public appearance with Prince Charles and Camilla, Duchess of Cornwall, at the Cheltenham Gold Cup.

December 2006
Catherine and her parents attend William's Sandhurst graduation.
December 2006
Jigsaw appoints Catherine as its accessories buyer.

14 April 2007
It is announced that the couple have split.

1 July 2007
The couple appear reunited after the Concert for Diana at Wembley.

21 July 2007
Catherine is invited to Camilla's 60th birthday party at Highgrove.

November 2007
Catherine quits her job at Jigsaw.

7 January 2008
William begins a four-month attachment at RAF Cranwell's flying school.

11 April 2008
Catherine watches as William receives his RAF "wings" from the Prince of Wales.

11 January 2009
William starts training at RAF Shawbury in Shropshire.

May 2009
William begins training as helicopter pilot at Shawbury.

5 December 2009
A crackdown on paparazzi fuels speculation about a royal engagement.

15 January 2010
William successfully completes his advanced helicopter training course.

October 2010
William proposes to Catherine on Kenyan safari holiday.

16 November 2010
The royal engagement is officially announced

December 2010
The couple make their first public engagement together for the Teenage Cancer Trust.

29 April 2011
William and Catherine marry at Westminster Abbey.

Mid-May 2011
The couple honeymoon in the Seychelles.

30 June 2011
The royal couple depart for a tour of Canada and the USA.

26 October 2011
Catherine makes her first solo engagement, hosting a charity dinner for In Kind Direct.

28 November 2011
William and Catherine take part in a media reception to mark the 2012 Diamond Jubilee.

31 December, 2011
The couple break with tradition by spending New Year with Catherine's parents.

2 February 2012
William arrives in the Falkland Islands for a six-week deployment.

8 March 2012
Catherine joins the Queen and Prince Philip on a visit to Leicester on the first day of the Queen's Diamond Jubilee tour.

17 March 2012
Catherine makes her first public speech, at a hospice in Suffolk.

2 June 2012
The Cambridges board the *Spirit of Chartwell* for the Diamond Jubilee river pageant.

July and August 2012
The couple support Team GB at the Olympics and Paralympics.

September 2012
William and Catherine represent the Queen on the Diamond Jubilee tour to Singapore, Malaysia, the Solomon Islands and Tuvalu.

3 December 2012
Catherine's first pregnancy is announced. She is said to be suffering from hyperemesis gravidarum and requires hospitalisation.

16 December 2012
Catherine makes her first public engagement after leaving King Edward VI hospital at the Sports Personality of the Year Awards.

4 June 2013
Catherine attends a Thanksgiving Service in Westminster Abbey to mark the 60th anniversary of the Queen's Coronation.

15 June 2013
Catherine attends the Trooping of the Colour – her final public engagement before the birth.

19 June 2013
An announcement is made that the royal baby will be born in the private Lindo Wing of St Mary's Hospital, Paddington, where William and Harry were born.

22 July 2013
Prince George Alexander Louis is born at 4.24pm weighing 8lbs 6oz (3.79kg).

August 2013
The first official portrait is taken of the new family in the garden of the Middleton home.

23 October 2013
Prince George is christened at Chapel Royal.

April 2014
William, Catherine and George embark on their tour of New Zealand and Australia.

2 July 2014
Prince George celebrates his first birthday.

8 September 2014
Clarence House releases a statement that tells the world that a second baby is due in April.

7 December 2014
William and Catherine go on whirl-wind trip to New York.

25 December 2014
The new royal family celebrate Christmas at Anmer Hall with Catherine's parents and siblings.

27 March 2015
The Duchess of Cambridge embarks on her last official engagements before going on "maternity leave".

2 May 2015
Princess Charlotte Elizabeth Diana is born at 8.34am, weighing 8lb 3oz (3.71kg).

WILLIAM'S FAMILY TREE

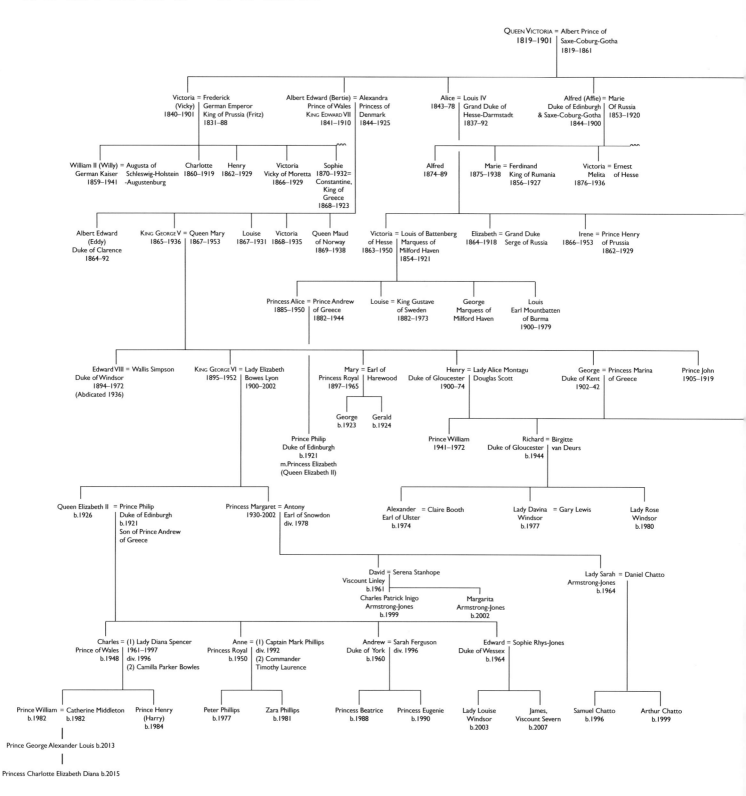

QUEEN VICTORIA = Albert Prince of
1819–1901 | Saxe-Coburg-Gotha
1819–1861

Victoria = Frederick
(Vicky) | German Emperor
1840–1901 | King of Prussia (Fritz)
1831–88

Albert Edward (Bertie) = Alexandra
Prince of Wales | Princess of
KING EDWARD VII | Denmark
1841–1910 | 1844–1925

Alice = Louis IV
1843–78 | Grand Duke of
Hesse-Darmstadt
1837–92

Alfred (Affie) = Marie
Duke of Edinburgh | Of Russia
& Saxe-Coburg-Gotha | 1853–1920
1844–1900

William II (Willy) = Augusta of
German Kaiser | Schleswig-Holstein
1859–1941 | -Augustenburg

Charlotte
1860–1919

Henry
1862–1929

Victoria
Vicky of Moretta
1866–1929

Sophie
1870–1932=
Constantine,
King of
Greece
1868–1923

Alfred
1874–89

Marie = Ferdinand
1875–1938 | King of Rumania
1856–1927

Victoria = Ernest
Melita | of Hesse
1876–1936

Albert Edward
(Eddy)
Duke of Clarence
1864–92

KING GEORGE V = Queen Mary
1865–1936 | 1867–1953

Louise
1867–1931

Victoria
1868–1935

Queen Maud
of Norway
1869–1938

Victoria = Louis of Battenberg
of Hesse | Marquess of
1863–1950 | Milford Haven
1854–1921

Elizabeth = Grand Duke
1864–1918 | Serge of Russia

Irene = Prince Henry
1866–1953 | of Prussia
1862–1929

Princess Alice = Prince Andrew
1885–1950 | of Greece
1882–1944

Louise = King Gustave
of Sweden
1882–1973

George
Marquess of
Milford Haven

Louis
Earl Mountbatten
of Burma
1900–1979

Edward VIII = Wallis Simpson
Duke of Windsor
1894–1972
(Abdicated 1936)

KING GEORGE VI = Lady Elizabeth
1895–1952 | Bowes Lyon
1900–2002

Mary = Earl of
Princess Royal | Harewood
1897–1965

Henry = Lady Alice Montagu
Duke of Gloucester | Douglas Scott
1900–74

George = Princess Marina
Duke of Kent | of Greece
1902–42

Prince John
1905–1919

George
b.1923

Gerald
b.1924

Prince Philip
Duke of Edinburgh
b.1921
m.Princess Elizabeth
(Queen Elizabeth II)

Prince William
1941–1972

Richard = Birgitte
Duke of Gloucester | van Deurs
b.1944

Queen Elizabeth II = Prince Philip
b.1926 | Duke of Edinburgh
b.1921
Son of Prince Andrew
of Greece

Princess Margaret = Antony
1930-2002 | Earl of Snowdon
div. 1978

Alexander = Claire Booth
Earl of Ulster
b.1974

Lady Davina = Gary Lewis
Windsor
b.1977

Lady Rose
Windsor
b.1980

David = Serena Stanhope
Viscount Linley
b.1961

Charles Patrick Inigo
Armstrong-Jones
b.1999

Margarita
Armstrong-Jones
b.2002

Lady Sarah = Daniel Chatto
Armstrong-Jones
b.1964

Charles = (1) Lady Diana Spencer
Prince of Wales | 1961–1997
b.1948 | div. 1996
(2) Camilla Parker Bowles

Anne = (1) Captain Mark Phillips
Princess Royal | div. 1992
b.1950 | (2) Commander
Timothy Laurence

Andrew = Sarah Ferguson
Duke of York | div. 1996
b.1960

Edward = Sophie Rhys-Jones
Duke of Wessex
b.1964

Prince William = Catherine Middleton
b.1982 | b.1982

Prince Henry
(Harry)
b.1984

Peter Phillips
b.1977

Zara Phillips
b.1981

Princess Beatrice
b.1988

Princess Eugenie
b.1990

Lady Louise
Windsor
b.2003

James,
Viscount Severn
b.2007

Samuel Chatto
b.1996

Arthur Chatto
b.1999

Prince George Alexander Louis b.2013

Princess Charlotte Elizabeth Diana b.2015

RIGHT: *The young Prince William with his parents, Prince Charles and Princess Diana.*

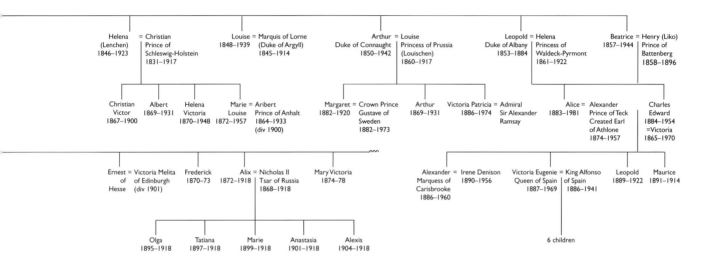

| Helena (Lenchen) 1846–1923 | = Christian Prince of Schleswig-Holstein 1831–1917 | | | Louise 1848–1939 | = Marquis of Lorne (Duke of Argyll) 1845–1914 | | Arthur Duke of Connaught 1850–1942 | = Louise Princess of Prussia (Louischen) 1860–1917 | | | Leopold Duke of Albany 1853–1884 | = Helena Princess of Waldeck-Pyrmont 1861–1922 | | Beatrice 1857–1944 | = Henry (Liko) Prince of Battenberg 1858–1896 |

| Christian Victor 1867–1900 | Albert 1869–1931 | Helena Victoria 1870–1948 | Marie Louise 1872–1957 | = Aribert Prince of Anhalt 1864–1933 (div 1900) | Margaret 1882–1920 | = Crown Prince Gustave of Sweden 1882–1973 | Arthur 1869–1931 | Victoria Patricia 1886–1974 | = Admiral Sir Alexander Ramsay | Alice 1883–1981 | = Alexander Prince of Teck Created Earl of Athlone 1874–1957 | Charles Edward 1884–1954 =Victoria 1865–1970 |

| Ernest of Hesse | = Victoria Melita of Edinburgh (div 1901) | Frederick 1870–73 | Alix 1872–1918 | = Nicholas II Tsar of Russia 1868–1918 | Mary Victoria 1874–78 | Alexander Marquess of Carisbrooke 1886–1960 | = Irene Denison 1890–1956 | Victoria Eugenie Queen of Spain 1887–1969 | = King Alfonso of Spain 1886–1941 | Leopold 1889–1922 | Maurice 1891–1914 |

| Olga 1895–1918 | Tatiana 1897–1918 | Marie 1899–1918 | Anastasia 1901–1918 | Alexis 1904–1918 | | 6 children |

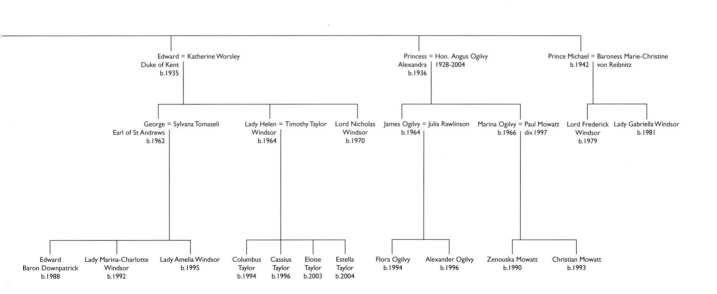

| Edward Duke of Kent b.1935 | = Katherine Worsley | | Princess Alexandra b.1936 | = Hon. Angus Ogilvy 1928-2004 | | Prince Michael b.1942 | = Baroness Marie-Christine von Reibnitz |

| George Earl of St Andrews b.1962 | = Sylvana Tomaseli | Lady Helen Windsor b.1964 | = Timothy Taylor | Lord Nicholas Windsor b.1970 | James Ogilvy b.1964 | = Julia Rawlinson | Marina Ogilvy b.1966 | = Paul Mowatt div.1997 | Lord Frederick Windsor b.1979 | Lady Gabriella Windsor b.1981 |

| Edward Baron Downpatrick b.1988 | Lady Marina-Charlotte Windsor b.1992 | Lady Amelia Windsor b.1995 | Columbus Taylor b.1994 | Cassius Taylor b.1996 | Eloise Taylor b.2003 | Estella Taylor b.2004 | Flora Ogilvy b.1994 | Alexander Ogilvy b.1996 | Zenouska Mowatt b.1990 | Christian Mowatt b.1993 |

CATHERINE'S FAMILY TREE

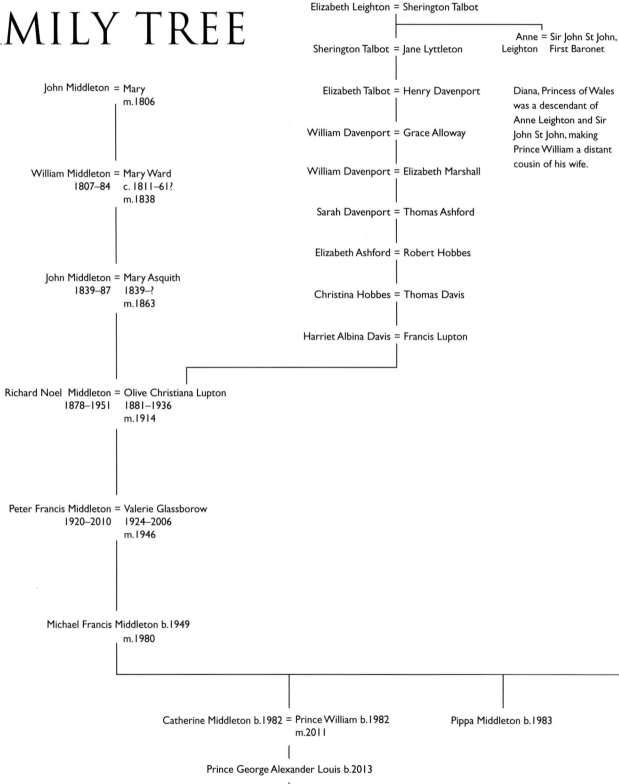

Sir Thomas Leighton = Elizabeth Knollys

Elizabeth Leighton = Sherington Talbot

Sherington Talbot = Jane Lyttleton

Anne = Sir John St John,
Leighton   First Baronet

John Middleton = Mary
m.1806

Elizabeth Talbot = Henry Davenport

Diana, Princess of Wales
was a descendant of
Anne Leighton and Sir
John St John, making
Prince William a distant
cousin of his wife.

William Davenport = Grace Alloway

William Middleton = Mary Ward
1807–84   c.1811–61?
m.1838

William Davenport = Elizabeth Marshall

Sarah Davenport = Thomas Ashford

John Middleton = Mary Asquith
1839–87   1839–?
m.1863

Elizabeth Ashford = Robert Hobbes

Christina Hobbes = Thomas Davis

Harriet Albina Davis = Francis Lupton

Richard Noel Middleton = Olive Christiana Lupton
1878–1951   1881–1936
m.1914

Peter Francis Middleton = Valerie Glassborow
1920–2010   1924–2006
m.1946

Michael Francis Middleton b.1949
m.1980

Catherine Middleton b.1982 = Prince William b.1982
m.2011

Pippa Middleton b.1983

Prince George Alexander Louis b.2013

Princess Charlotte Elizabeth Diana b.2015

10

BELOW: *Pippa Middleton and Catherine attend the wedding of Sam Waley-Cohen and Annabel Ballin at St Michael and All Angels Church on 11 June 2011 in Lambourn, Berkshire, near the Middletons' home.*

John Goldsmith = Rebecca Wheeler
c.1783–1851? c.1796–1869
m. ?

John Goldsmith = Esther Jones
c.1827–1888 c. 1832–1885
m.1850

John Goldsmith = Jane Dorsett
1851- 1861–?
m.1882

Stephen Charles Goldsmith = Edith Eliza Chandler
1886–1938 1889–1971
m.1909

Ronald John James Goldsmith = Dorothy Harrison
1931–2003 1935–2006
m.1953

Carole Elizabeth Goldsmith b.1955

James Middleton b.1987

TWO VERY DIFFERENT CHILDHOODS

June 1982 proved to be an eventful month for the royal family. Pope John Paul II ended his visit to Britain by asking God to "bestow abundant blessings on Your Majesty"; US President Ronald Reagan, on an official visit to the UK, enjoyed an early morning horse ride with the Queen at Windsor; helicopter pilot Prince Andrew was safe and sound in the Falkland Islands as Argentine forces surrendered; and the Queen Mother welcomed home the QE2 and her 629 troops on board. Meanwhile at St Mary's Hospital, Paddington, on 21 June HRH The Princess of Wales gave birth to a 7lb 1½ oz baby boy.

LEFT: *Proud parents Prince Charles and Princess Diana leave St Mary's hospital on 22 June 1982 lovingly craddling their new born son William.*

In the early autumn of 1981 Diana knew that she was pregnant, and would be the first Princess of Wales to have a baby in nearly 80 years. William Arthur Philip Louis was born at 9.03 pm, 16 hours after Diana had been admitted. A crowd of photographers, film crews and well-wishers built up during the day. When news of the birth broke, so did a rendition of "Rule Britannia", followed by "Nice One Charlie… let's have another one".

A letter written by the proud father a few days later to Countess Mountbatten of Burma, suggests that Charles was still mesmerized by the whole experience. "The arrival of our small son has been an astonishing experience and one that has meant more to me than I ever could have imagined…. I am so thankful I was beside Diana's bedside the whole time because by the end of the day I really felt as though I'd shared deeply in the process of birth and as a result was rewarded by seeing a small creature which belonged to us even though he seemed to belong to everyone else as well!"

The fact that the "small creature" was public property was emphasized by the media in the aftermath of his birth. "The birth of an heir is a national landmark," announced *The Times*, adding, "it is a constitutional as well as a joyous, private occasion."

Home for the newborn prince was an L-shaped apartment in Kensington Palace, newly renovated by South African designer Dudley Poplak. The nursery on the top floor comprised three bedrooms, a playroom, a kitchen and a dining room, and would be William's home for the ensuing 15 years.

Prince Harry was born on 15 September 1984 when William was just two. Any fear of sibling rivalry was quickly dispelled as Diana noted to a friend, "William adores his little brother and spends the entire time pouring an endless supply of hugs and kisses on Harry, and we are hardly allowed near."

Unfortunately the angelic phase was short lasting. By the time he was four William was creating havoc, once trying to flush his father's shoe down the lavatory and another time setting off the alarms on the Queen's Balmoral estate, resulting in police cars hurtling in from Aberdeen to seal off the grounds.

In September 1985, aged three he was sent to Mrs Mynors' Nursery School in Notting Hill Gate where his final report card, now in the Royal Archives, tells us that "Prince William was very popular with the other children, and was known for his kindness, sense of fun, and quality of thoughtfulness".

After 15 months, the prince moved on to nearby Wetherby School, where he would stay for the next three years. He was noted for his flair in English and spelling and proved he had inherited his mother's love of swimming by winning the Grunfield Cup for the best overall swimming style.

More sporting success followed at Ludgrove Preparatory School in Berkshire where he studied for five years. William was captain of the hockey and football teams and represented the school in cross-country running. It was while he was at Ludgrove that his parents announced their separation in December 1992.

ABOVE: *Queen Elizabeth II watches a polo match with her grandsons Prince William and Prince Harry in June 1987.*

RIGHT: *The Prince and Princess of Wales pose with William and Harry on the steps of the Spanish royal residence Marivent Palace on the island of Majorca during a family holiday in August 1987.*

The week before the announcement, Diana drove to Ludgrove to break the news of the separation to her sons. William, although only ten, took the news stoically and said, "I hope you will both be happy now."

Diana was keen that William should respect his royal heritage. Initially, she maintained a warm association with her former mother-in-law, telling one friend, "It's very important to me that my sons have a very good relationship with the Queen." She also hated criticism of Charles by third parties: "The princess never liked that sort of thing and would rebuke them saying, 'Remember that he's the father of my children,'" recalled her friend Roberto Devorik.

Under the terms of the separation the two princes would now divide their weekends away between Diana at Kensington Palace and Charles at Highgrove House in Gloucestershire.

Weekends with the princess often involved treats – from burgers at McDonalds in Kensington High Street to white-knuckle rides at Alton Towers in Staffordshire. There were also visits to Disney World in Florida, holidays in the Caribbean and white water rafting in Colorado.

At Highgrove, William grew accustomed to country pursuits from an early age. The 348 acres of parkland were perfect for bike rides, skateboarding and riding his Shetland pony away from the prying eyes of the public. Later he enjoyed shooting and stalking with his father on the Queen's estates, as well as polo – Charles bought him a polo pony for his 17th birthday.

BELOW: *One of the most memorable trips Princess Diana took with her boys was to Alton Towers in 1994. Here they can be seen enjoying the log flume ride at the amusement park.*

LEFT: *Prince Harry shares a comment with his elder brother, much to their mother's amusement. Along with Princes Charles, they were attending the VJ Day commemorations staged outside Buckingham Palace in August 1995. The event, which marked the 60th anniversary of victory over Japan in the Second World War, was attended by 15,000 veterans and tens of thousands of spectators*

In July 1997 a helicopter landed in the grounds of Kensington Palace to take Diana, William and Harry on what would turn out to be their final holiday together. Mohamed Al Fayed, the Egyptian-born owner of Harrods International, had invited them to stay on his yacht *Jonikal* which then headed for St Tropez where the family owned a villa. It was during this cruise that Diana was introduced to Al Fayed's 42-year-old son, Dodi. The two began a highly publicized affair that tragically ended with their deaths in an horrific car crash in Paris just six weeks later.

The young princes were staying at Balmoral Castle with their father when Diana died. Both Charles and the Queen were woken in the early hours of the morning when news of the accident was forwarded from Buckingham Palace. The prince decided to let his sons sleep on until 7.30 when they normally awoke. Fifteen minutes later he went to their adjoining rooms to break the news to them that their mother was dead.

During the days that followed William and Harry showed remarkable self-control and maturity beyond their years; indeed, they faced the cameras less than four hours after hearing the news when they attended a church service at Crathie Kirk. Later in the week they again remained composed when they took flowers from well-wishers in the grounds of Kensington Palace, while across London their grandmother paid a television tribute to Diana praising "her energy and commitment to others, especially her two boys".

The following day the two princes stood shoulder to shoulder with their father, their grandfather Prince Philip, and their uncle Earl Spencer as Diana's cortège slowly moved into view along the Mall. Under the gaze of thousands of onlookers, the boys walked behind their mother's coffin.

Diana once said that William and Harry were the only two men who had never let her down and in the years that followed they have continued to protect her memory and her legacy.

Charles now reconstructed his work and leisure time so that his world could revolve around his two young sons. After their first Christmas without

their mother, he took them to Klosters for a week's skiing. On their return, he announced that he would be "streamlining" his charities in order to spend more time with them. The boys joined him in March 1998 for a visit to British Columbia in Canada during which William was given a rapturous welcome from thousands of Vancouver's teenagers.

In June of 1998, nine days before his 16th birthday, William was finally introduced to Camilla Parker Bowles, the woman who would eventually become his stepmother, at St James's Palace. The two had what was later called "a cordial and general discussion about all manner of things."

In the summer of 1998 William passed nine GCSEs with A grades in English, History and Languages. He had already passed three others the previous year, and the royal family was said to be "privately delighted" that William had been so successful despite the trauma of his mother's death.

In his final two years at Eton, William won the Sword of Honour as best cadet in the Eton College Officer Training Corps. He was also elected a member of Pop, the college's élite group of 19 prefects responsible for supervising the other 1,260 boys.

The prince's A Level passes – an A grade in Geography, a B in History and a C in Biology – confirmed his status as one of the brightest royals. It also meant that he gained his university place at St Andrews on merit rather than favouritism.

Charles was keen that his son should take a year off before continuing his academic career so he opted to join 15 other volunteers for a ten-week Raleigh International project in the remote community of Tortel, deep in the heart of the Andes. During this year he also joined his father's regiment, the Welsh Guards, to take part in training exercises in the jungles of Belize. Then in September 2000 he headed for Mauritius to carry out an educational programme with the Royal Geographical Society.

Ironically, given the vast amount of travel and the exotic locations, William's favourite part of his year off was the short time he spent much closer to home. "The best bit was in England," he told a journalist before starting at university. "I loved working on a farm, before foot and mouth, which is why I've got so much sympathy for the farmers who have suffered so much from it. It was the best part of my year. I got my hands dirty, did all the chores, and had to get up 4.00 am. I got to see a completely different lifestyle."

Having stretched himself physically it was now time for William to resume his academic career. Aged 19, he said that he had little idea what the next four years would hold; he couldn't know that he was about to meet the woman who would one day become his wife.

Despite coming from very different backgrounds, there is a familial link between William and Catherine. Both are related to Sir Thomas Leighton, an Elizabethan soldier, diplomat and for 40 years the Governor of Guernsey. He is the prince's 12th generation great-grandparent and Catherine's 11th, making them

ABOVE: *This photograph, part of an official series released by St James Palace in June 2000 to mark the Prince's 18th birthday, shows William playing in a football match at Eton.*

LEFT: *William proudly poses in his Eton uniform.*

12th cousins once removed. Catherine and William are also both descended from King Edward III, famed for his crushing victory over the French at the Battle of Crécy in 1346.

Among Catherine's other antecedents are Harriet Martineau, cited as the first woman sociologist and there are vague connections between other writers and Catherine's family. She is a distant cousin of the children's author Beatrix Potter, and is also related to Arthur Ransome, who produced *Swallows and Amazons*. Ransome's sister Joyce was married to Hugo Lupton, the cousin of Catherine's great-grandmother Olive. The Luptons, Catherine's ancestors on her father's side, were comfortably-off stalwarts of Leeds society in the late 19th and early 20th centuries.

On her mother's side Catherine's ancestors were of solid working-class stock. For instance James Harrison, who started work as a miner in the coalfields of County Durham in 1819.

The fortunes of Catherine's family were to change again radically as recently as the 1980s thanks to the hard work of her parents, Michael and Carole. The couple had met in the 1970s when they both worked for British Airways (BA). After dating for several years, they set up home in the Berkshire village of Bradfield Southend. They married eight months later in June 1980.

Catherine Elizabeth Middleton was born on 9 January 1982 at the Royal Berkshire Hospital at Reading. Her younger sister Philippa, known as Pippa, was born at the same hospital 20 months later on 6 September 1985, and their only

ABOVE: *On a March 1998 visit to Vancouver, Canada, with his father and brother, William shows his impish side – having been presented with Canadian Olympic jackets and baseball caps, William decides to put his hat on back to front.*

brother, James William, was born in April 1987 when Catherine was five.

For the first 13 years of Catherine's life the family lived in the village of Bradfield Southend. At the age of four Catherine started at the local school, Bradfield Church of England Primary School. Here the future princess showed a healthy interest in sport and also passed her cycling proficiency test. She has remained a keen cyclist ever since and was often spotted biking to lectures at St Andrews.

Michael Middleton was still working for BA, but Carole, with three children to look after, also found time to make party bags which she sold to other mums while Catherine was still a toddler. This seed of an idea eventually germinated into Party Pieces which Carole founded around the time of James's birth.

In the autumn of 1989, Catherine was sent to the co-educational St Andrew's School in Pangbourne, four miles from home. Again, she excelled at sport, winning swimming races and joining the netball team. She was also good at the high jump and broke the school record for her age group.

Catherine was also keen on amateur theatricals, starring in the school production of the Tchaikovsky ballet *The Nutcracker* and taking the role of Eliza Doolittle

BELOW: *Like her future husband, Catherine also enjoyed playing sports at school. In this photograph of the St Andrew's School hockey team, Catherine appears in the centre of the front row. On 30 November 2012, Catherine returned to visit her old school and met the current members of the hockey team.*

in *My Fair Lady*. In her final year she starred as the heroine in a Victorian melodrama, which was videoed at the time and has since been on several TV documentaries mainly because her love interest in the play was called William.

In July 1995, when Catherine was 13, the family moved to its present home on the outskirts of Chapel Row, in the parish of Bucklebury and the following April Catherine arrived at Marlborough School. Several friends from her Marlborough days have given newspaper interviews and none of them has a bad word to say about Catherine. Thankfully for Catherine's present role, there seem to be few, if any, skeletons in her cupboard.

Catherine passed her 11 GCSEs with flying colours. She returned the following term to begin her A level studies and friends noticed a change that summer of 1998. "She came back an absolute beauty," remembers Gemma Williamson. "She never wore particularly fashionable or revealing clothes – just jeans and a jumper – but she had an innate sense of style."

Catherine's time at Marlborough paid off and in her A Levels she gained A grades in Mathematics and Art as well as a B in English.

Like William, the next stage for Catherine was a year off. Two months after graduating, she stayed in Florence where she immersed herself in the city's rich legacy of paintings and sculptures. Arriving in September 2000, she studied Italian for 12 weeks in a class of a dozen girls at the British Institute. She shared a flat above an Italian delicatessen with a group that included singer Chris Rea's niece, Alice Whitaker.

ABOVE: *During her time at St Andrew's School in Pangbourne, Berkshire, Catherine excelled at a number of sports including tennis, swimming, netball, hockey and rounders. Catherine, pictured in the middle of the front row, was the highest scorer on the under-12/13 rounders team.*

After Florence, Catherine joined Raleigh International, co-incidentally the same organization that William had joined. Like the prince, she went to Chile, though not on the same expedition; hers was in the spring of 2001, several months after William had returned.

Malcolm Sutherland from Ross-shire, who worked for Raleigh International at the time, met them both and recalls, "For ten weeks each lived with absolutely no luxuries. This was roughing it by anyone's standards.

"Kate's trip involved three weeks of trekking, three weeks on a marine survey and her remaining weeks on a community.

"There was absolutely no connection between the couple at that stage and it's an incredible coincidence that they chose the same company and the same organization, but I think it shows how well suited William and Kate are."

Malcolm feels they will make a great couple: "She's an incredibly straightforward down-to-earth girl. I think she'd be supportive to William but not subservient. She's a modern girl, hugely intelligent and fun. I think she's exactly what the monarchy needs."

Kate's family tree with its emphasis on hard work, community service and moral integrity, down through the generations, has reached fruition in Kate. The confidence she gained from her close-knit family, her academic success, her love of sport and her faultless personality would all equip her to face her next stage in life – university.

ABOVE: *At the age of 13 Catherine went to Marlborough School. A schoolmate has since revealed that Catherine kept a poster of Prince William in her dorm room and said – perhaps in jest – that she would one day marry him.*

A Low Key Courtship

As William prepared to begin four years of study at St Andrews, he was heard to say "I just want to go to university to have fun. I want to go there and be an ordinary student. I mean, I'm only going to university. It's not like I'm getting married".

LEFT: *Catherine and William pose together at their graduation ceremony on 23 June 2005.*

William's words seem ironic now, but little did he realize in 2001 that the path to academic success would also lead to the altar. On his arrival at St Andrews, in September 2001 William was warmly greeted by an enthusiastic crowd of 3,000 locals and 100 photographers. Blushing strongly, William looked awkward as fans and well-wishers cheered his arrival. However, university is a great social leveller, and once he had dropped his royal title he soon melted into the background.

Making friends when you are a prince isn't easy, though William was confident of his ability to gauge true characters No doubt he was as astute when it came to meeting women. During his time in his halls of residence, William kept bumping into the same attractive brunette, Catherine Middleton. They shared a halls of residence, were on the same course (at least before William switched to Geography) and both loved sport. However, their relationship was strictly platonic, as Catherine was dating fourth-year student Rupert Finch.

It was during his second term that cupid's dart hit William one evening at the end of March 2002. It was the night of the annual Don't Walk charity fashion show and the prince had paid £200 for his front-row seat. His eyes nearly popped out of his head when Catherine walked down the catwalk wearing a see-through dress and black underwear. Afterwards there was a party at a student house, and William made his move, engaging Catherine in a long conversation before leaning in for a kiss. Catherine, who was still dating Rupert, rebuffed him.

In the autumn of the same year, Catherine was one of a party of 16 friends, including the prince, who stayed at Wood Farm on the Queen's Sandringham estate for a shooting weekend. Long-lens photos of the group taken by local photographers show Catherine wreathed in smiles standing next to the prince. It was the first time that the couple had appeared in the same frame and inevitably fuelled speculation that this young lady was "the one".

In May 2003 the couple were again snapped unawares, this time deep in conversation at a rugby sevens match. The same month Catherine's father gave a good-natured rebuttal to a journalist's suggestion that his daughter might be dating the future king. "I spoke to Catherine just a few days ago," said Michael, "and I can categorically confirm they are no more than good friends." A month later, William celebrated his 21st birthday with an "Out of Africa" themed party at Windsor Castle. His uncles, Earl Spencer and the Duke of York, were dressed as big-game hunters and his grandmother was dressed as her African counterpart the Queen of Swaziland, complete with tribal headdress. "I thought it would be fun to see the family out of black ties and get everyone to dress up," he told an interviewer a few days earlier.

There was no mention of Catherine in the following day's newspapers as the headlines were dominated by news of the arrest of an intruder, Aaron Barschak, a self-styled "comedy terrorist" who gatecrashed the event.

The second noteworthy event picked up on was the presence of Jessica Craig, known to her friends as "Jecca", whose family owned a 45,000-acre reserve

ABOVE: *Prince William graduates from St Andrews with a 2:1 in Geography.*

LEFT: *William and his father walk around St Andrews on William's first day as a student there on 23 September 2001.*

in Kenya that William has visited on several occasions. After the Windsor party the prince took the unusual step of denying the romance with Jecca. His spokeswoman announced, "St James's Palace denies that there is or ever has been any romantic liaison between Prince William and Jessica Craig." In an interview to mark his milestone birthday, William flatly denied that romance was on the horizon with Catherine, Jecca or anybody else. "There's been a lot of speculation about every single girl I'm with, and it actually does quite irritate me after a while, more so because it's a complete pain for the girls".

The exact date when William and Catherine's friendship developed into a romance remains uncertain, though it is thought to have been some time towards the end of 2003.

It was the following Easter, in April 2004, that it became obvious they were a couple. Paparazzo Jason Fraser, who had broken the news of the Diana and Dodi romance by photographing them kissing on the Al Fayed yacht *Jonikal*, snapped a series of photos of William and Catherine in a chairlift at the ski resort of Klosters. The couple are staring fondly at each other and the next morning's *Sun* newspaper carried the photo and the headline: "FINALLY… WILLS GETS A GIRL".

There were few public sightings of the couple during the next year. Catherine wasn't invited to the wedding of Prince Charles to Camilla Parker Bowles in April 2005, probably because her presence in front of the world's media would have fuelled expectation that theirs would be the next royal marriage.

Two weeks before the wedding Charles, William and Harry had returned to Klosters for a genteel version of a stag do. On their first night of their Swiss holiday William took the unusual step of having a 30-minute informal chat with journalists during which he spoke about marriage – or the lack of one in his case. "Look, I'm only 22 for God's sake," he told the hacks. "I'm too young to marry at my age. I don't want to get married until I'm at least 28 or maybe 30."

The prince was 28 when he walks down the aisle, so his 2005 casual interview proved to be prescient.

In June 2005 William and Catherine attended the wedding of Hugh van Cutsem and Rose Astor at St John's Church in Burford, Oxfordshire. Hugh's parents, Emilie and Hugh senior, are old friends of the Prince of Wales and he and his three brothers, Edward, Nicholas and William, have known William and Harry since the latter were born. As would be their regular practice at the many weddings they have attended over the past five years, William and Catherine arrived separately, with a smiling Catherine running the gauntlet of photographers as she entered the 12th-century building. Only later did the couple meet up at Bruern, the Astor home, where they danced intimately together before leaving for a romantic stay at the King's Head in Bledington.

After their graduation in June 2005 there was another romantic break, this time in Kenya. Again there was a separate arrival, with William jetting in from New Zealand following an official tour. It was William's third visit to Lewa

BELOW: *Catherine looking effortlessly beautiful at her graduation where she was awarded a 2:1 degree in Art History.*

Downs, which had been home to Jecca Craig's family since they emigrated there after the First World War. If Catherine had had any reservations about William's relationship with their host's daughter they were dispelled during this break during which they were joined by Jecca's new boyfriend, financier Hugh Crossley.

Back in the UK, Catherine found herself hounded by the press. In October 2005, following the publication of a photo showing her looking out of the window of a London bus the previous month, her lawyers, the same used by the Prince of Wales, asked newspaper and magazine editors to respect her privacy. Her legal team claimed that photographers had followed her almost every day and night since she left university.

That autumn there were rumours that the relationship had cooled off, but in November William put paid to those when he discussed Catherine at a Buckingham Palace reception for the visiting New Zealand All Blacks rugby team when he told the lock forward Ali Williams that their relationship was "going well, going steady".

In January, the couple were once again skiing in Klosters. Despite knowing there must have been cameras spying on their every move in the popular resort, William planted a kiss on Catherine's cheek and, sure enough, the photo was splashed across the front pages.

Days later William began his army training at the Royal Military Academy, Sandhurst, and the romance was virtually on hold yet again. This earned his

ABOVE: *The Queen looks proud after attending William's gradutation. William's graduation was an opportunity for the Queen to catch her first glimpse of the girl who had captured her grandson's heart.*

LEFT: *William takes a moment to speak to his father Prince Charles following his graduation.*

RIGHT: *Catherine looking thrilled to be joining the royal ski party on their trip to Klosters in Switzerland in March 2005.*

FAR LEFT: *William can't help but smile as he is inspected by his grandmother, Queen Elizabeth II during The Sovereign's Parade at The Royal Military Academy Sandhurst on 15 December 2006.*

LEFT: *Catherine looks on while William takes part in The Sovereign's Parade. In total, 446 Officer Cadets took part in the parade and the armed forces of 14 different countries were represented.*

girlfriend the title "Waity Katie" for her seemingly endless ability to stand by her man, and put her own future on hold while his progressed steadily.

The pair met up the weekend before Valentine's Day, but the break ended up as something of a disaster after they joined William's cousins Peter and Zara Phillips and William's old friend Guy Pelly for a night out. The group met at the Tunnel House Inn, in the village of Coates, near Cirencester, a 15-minute drive from Highgrove. Pelly was secretly filmed smoking cannabis, which he denied possessing, saying that he had been offered it by a girl in the pub and had thought it was a cigarette. William and Catherine weren't involved but there were questions raised about the company they were keeping.

In March, Catherine arrived on her own to watch National Hunt's most prestigious race, the Cheltenham Gold Cup. In a telling gesture, she was invited to the Royal Box for lunch with Prince Charles and the Duchess of Cornwall and was later photographed with the royal party on the balcony overlooking the racecourse. It was the first time she had been seen in public with her future in-laws and, given that Prince William wasn't even present, it was a sign that she was definitely part of the family. Later in the day she watched the races with Camilla's children Tom and Laura and their partners.

There was another sign the romance was blossoming when Catherine turned up at Eton College to watch William play in the old boys' Eton Field Game match. She embraced him in front of guests and playfully ruffled his thinning locks.

A month later, the couple flew to Mustique which had been a favourite holiday destination of the prince's great aunt Princess Margaret. William and Catherine plus a group of friends stayed in a five-bedroomed villa belonging to Belle and John Robinson the owners of the Jigsaw fashion chain. While they were there they met up with Richard Branson and played several games of tennis with the Virgin Group boss, whose daughter Holly is a friend of the royal couple. They also went to Firefly, a fashionable guesthouse, where Zara Phillips has stayed, and ordered cocktails. Another holidaymaker said, "They were very nice and ordinary. They watched the sunset and had two drinks each, signing them to the Villa Hibiscus account."

The couple also visited Basil's Bar, a local bistro that was a great favourite of Margaret's. "On karaoke night the prince and two of his friends sang Elvis Presley's 'Suspicious Minds'," a staff member later recalled. "The prince drank his favourite vodka and cranberry juice while Catherine enjoyed a piña colada flavoured with St Vincent's own blend of rum, Sunset Premium."

On their return, they attended the Wiltshire wedding of Camilla's daughter Laura to Harry Lopes, grandson of the late Lord Astor of Hever. As usual, Catherine arrived after William, but her presence at a family wedding once again fuelled speculation that a more royal one was imminent.

BELOW: *Catherine leaving her home in Chelsea in London on her 25th birthday surrounded by photographers.*

During the second half of the year, Catherine was devastated by the loss of her two grandmothers, Carole's mother Dorothy Goldsmith succumbed to cancer in July at the age of 71 and Catherine read a poem at her funeral. Then Michael's mother Valerie died from lymphoma in September at the age of 82. Her widower Peter died just a week before William and Catherine announced their engagement in November 2010.

To cheer Catherine up, William arranged for them to charter a yacht with some friends off the holiday island of Ibiza. Photos show them happy and relaxed as they dived into the sea, and at one point they all appear to be enjoying a mud bath.

In December 2006, Catherine and her parents and brother James were William's guests at his graduation ceremony at Sandhurst that was also attended by Charles, Camilla, Prince Philip and the Queen. Instead of walking from the car park with other families, Catherine's party walked down the ceremonial routeway that was lined with troops for Her Majesty's arrival. It was the highest profile event that Catherine had attended so far and was seen as proof that the royal romance was rock solid.

No one watching that day could have realized that behind the public smiles their love affair was in fact starting to flounder and that four months later the couple would separate.

ABOVE: *Looking close, Prince William and Catherine watch the RBS Six Nations Championship rugby match between England and Italy at Twickenham a couple of months before their split; Prince Harry, meanwhile, appears somewhat non-plussed.*

BREAK UP & FIRMER FOOTING

Speculation of an imminent engagement had been rife since November 2006 when the now defunct British High Street chain Woolworths produced a range of memorabilia, including plates, mugs, thimbles and mouse mats, to mark the event.

LEFT: *Prince William and Prince Harry at the Concert for Diana held at Wembley Stadium on 1 July 2007. The Concert was held on what would have been the late Princess's 46th birthday and marked 10 years since her death. Catherine can be seen on the far right of the picture.*

In the New Year, the rumours gathered momentum as Catherine's 25th birthday approached on 9 January. Diana's former Private Secretary, wrote a feature for *The Spectator* entitled "The Next People's Princess" in which he suggested that the royal family was about to get "a much-needed injection of fresh young glamour".

Catherine was used to one or two photographers waiting to snap her as she left her Chelsea flat, but on the morning of her birthday there were dozens outside, awaiting an announcement. For William it was all too reminiscent of the hounding his mother had received in the run-up to her marriage, and his office issued a statement condemning the harassment Catherine.

William was now based with the Household Cavalry at Combermere Barracks in Windsor. There were the occasional meetings with Catherine in London but much of the spark had gone out of the relationship.

The couple booked a holiday in the exclusive Swiss resort of Zermatt, but William invited along some of his friends and Catherine found it frustrating that they now had no opportunity to be alone to talk things through.

Things got worse on their return when they attended the first day of the Cheltenham Festival in March 2007 and photographs from the event show Catherine with a forced smile and William looking distinctly out of sorts. Three days later, William moved to Dorset to begin a ten-week tank-commander course at Bovington army training camp. It was too far for him to visit the capital regularly at weekends, but it didn't stop him letting his hair down with his new army buddies.

William and Catherine's final night out together was a quiet one with friends Hugh and Rose van Cutsem, whose wedding in Burford they had attended in 2005. The four enjoyed a drink in the King's Head pub in Bledington. The couple's last meeting together after this was during the Easter weekend when they finally decided to call it a day.

The Sunday newspapers analysed what could have gone wrong, with many of them unfairly highlighting the Middleton family's middle-class background as a possible reason.

This period in their relationship, unsurprisingly, seems to have had a profound effect on them, and they spoke about it openly and at length during their interview with Tom Bradby on the day of their engagement. Catherine admitted that she had been angry about it at the time but she said that she now looked back on it as a positive experience and admitted she had been "consumed" with the relationship. The Prince said they had needed "space" at the time but he had always known Catherine was "very special".

In June 2007 the couple got back together after William had invited her to an end-of-training party in his barracks. The first the world at large knew of the rekindled romance was at the Concert for Diana, held at Wembley Stadium. A snatched photo of them shows them deep in conversation, over a candle-lit supper. The message was clear: the romance was back on.

ABOVE: *Wearing a regimental tie and traditional bowler hat, Prince William attends the Cavalry Old Comrades Association Annual Parade in London's Hyde Park in May 2007.*

LEFT: *Catherine appearing to be still upset in April 2007 following her break up with Prince William.*

LEFT: *Joining in on a joke together with friends, Catherine and William enjoy the polo on his 26th birthday.*

Any doubts that the royal romance was back on were dispelled later in the month when Catherine was invited to Camilla's 60th birthday party at Highgrove.

Camilla had been keen to invite her all along as she had always got on well with Catherine, but it had to be William's decision in the end. The prince was adamant that she should be there but he was equally determined not to upstage his step-mother's big day, so Catherine was smuggled in through a private driveway to the estate.

Catherine wore a stunning full-length cream dress and appeared happy and relaxed as she sipped champagne in the beautiful gardens. The 200 guests enjoyed a three-course organic dinner, and after speeches they took to the dance floor. Catherine was said to be "draped" over her boyfriend of four years, and William mouthed the words of the Frank Sinatra classic "It Had to Be You" to his girlfriend.

The same month that she was the belle of Camilla's ball, Catherine was named the most sought-after party guest in town by *Tatler*.

It was also during this year that Catherine began to receive plaudits for her fashion sense, and there were, and continue to be, obvious parallels drawn with the woman who would have been Catherine's mother-in-law. In July 2006, UK *Vogue* editor Alexandra Shulman wrote, "Catherine is a contemporary version of Princess Diana. She has the same mainstream style and will go on like Diana to get more glamorous."

For the House of Windsor, it is a plus that Catherine also plays it safe in the sartorial stakes. Her style is as discreet as her personality: attractive, classy, always appropriate for the occasion and with just the hint of quirkiness.

Both women took fashion advice to improve their look: Diana from *Vogue's* Anna Harvey and Catherine from stylist Leesa Whisker.

As future Queen, Catherine would be a terrific asset to the fashion industry if she followed the traditional Buy British route that royal ladies have favoured. Esteemed fashion director of the *Daily Telegraph* Hilary Alexander said, "Hopefully she will come out of the closet and be an ambassador for fashion. It would be great if she adopted young designers such as Richard Nicoll, Jonathan Saunders or Christopher Kane. Someone with her profile could give British fashion a boost across the world."

In August, the couple holidayed on Desroches Island, in the Seychelles. It was an opportunity for the two to be alone – apart from the inevitable personal detectives – in what would be their first overseas holiday since January 2006. Here it is believed that the couple made a pact. Catherine needed reassurance that the romance was going places, and William needed to know that he could concentrate on his career – he still had to spend another six months' deployment with the RAF and the Royal Navy. Marriage would be on the cards, but it would be a way off.

BELOW: *Prince William is awarded his flying wings from his father Prince Charles at his graduation from RAF Cranwell on 11 April 2008.*

Back in the UK, William had to put the finishing touches to the memorial service held at Wellington Barracks on 31 August 2007, to mark the tenth anniversary of his mother's death. Catherine didn't attend and, after a vitriolic war of words in the media, Camilla was also absent on the day. It was an intense occasion for Diana's sons. Prince Harry gave a moving address, telling the packed congregation, "When she was alive we completely took for granted her unrivalled love of life, laughter, fun and folly." In a voice breaking with emotion, he added, "She will always be remembered for her amazing public work. But behind the media glare, to us, she was quite simply the best mother in the world."

In a gesture that would have delighted Diana, William sat with the royal family, while Harry sat on the right side of the church with the Spencers, a healing gesture after a decade of division that began with Earl Spencer's funeral eulogy which captured the public mood at the time, but which went against the royal grain of keeping feelings buttoned up and private.

The long-awaited inquest into the deaths of Diana, Princess of Wales and Dodi Al Fayed opened on 2 October 2007. For William and Harry it must have been traumatic since it dealt with questions such as "Was Diana pregnant at the time of her death?" and "Were the British security services involved in her death?"

The day after, William and Catherine were spotted enjoying a dinner date in Locanda Ottoemezzo, a few hundred yards from his childhood home at Kensington Palace. For once there were no friends there, the ever-present paparazzi hadn't been tipped off about it, and the prince's detectives sat outside in a car to give the couple more privacy. They sat side by side at a small table, their faces close together in the candlelight, and at one point William cradled Catherine's face in his hands as they chatted in low voices.

A couple of days later the two were photographed together leaving Boujis nightclub at 2.00 am. For the photographers waiting outside it was a golden opportunity to snap the media-avoiding pair together and they chased William's Range Rover as it set off from Thurloe Street in South Kensington back to Clarence House. Given that it was the week in which the Diana inquest was examining the car chase that lead to her death, this episode was all the more upsetting for the prince.

Less than a week after the Press contretemps outside Boujis, Catherine was again snapped by the paparazzi, this time in Scotland, when she and the prince stayed with Prince Charles at Birkhall. Catherine proved that, unlike Diana who hated being "dragged" to the Deeside estate, she was really at home with the royal family's shooting, hunting and fishing lifestyle. Wearing a camouflage jacket, dark jeans, leg warmers and gaiters over her boots, she could be seen at one point lying on the ground preparing the sights of her gun before firing. The Prince of Wales, dressed in a waterproof jacket, stood nearby supervising proceedings.

The intimate family scene once again fuelled talk of an engagement.

ABOVE: *Showing to the world that they were very much a couple again, William and Catherine arrive at the Central Flying School at RAF Cranwell for the Prince's graduation.*

RIGHT: *On the final day of his unofficial visit to Australia in January 2010, Prince William arrives at Government House to a mass of adoring fans and wannabe princesses – it was the first time William had returned to Australia since going there with his parents when he was just nine months old.*

CAREERS

———————

Catherine celebrated her 26th birthday, as she had the previous one, without her boyfriend. In 2007 William had been on duty with the Household Cavalry. A year later, he was serving with the RAF at Cranwell.

———————

LEFT: *William and Harry enjoying a visit to a child education centre in Lesotho during their trip to South Africa in June 2010. During this trip, the brothers visited projects supported by their respective charities (Sentebale for Prince Harry and Tusk Trust for Prince William) and ended their trip by watching England vs Algeria during the World Cup in Cape Town.*

ABOVE: *Fashion brand Jigsaw's headquarters in Kew, west London. After less than a year Catherine quit her job as an accessories buyer – a role that had been specially created for her.*

As King William V, he will one day be Head of the Armed Services and during his apprenticeship years he was determined to serve in all three branches. On 7 January 2008, after seeing in the New Year with Catherine on the Balmoral estate, the prince arrived at the base to begin his four-month attachment to Cranwell's Central Flying School. Two days later, Catherine marked her birthday by visiting Tom Aikens' restaurant in Elystan Street, Chelsea with her parents and sister Pippa.

In March, Catherine made her third appearance at the Cheltenham Festival in as many years. It was exactly 12 months since her unhappy appearance with William had heralded the temporary end of their relationship. Now she was back looking chic with a navy blue raincoat and matching trilby as she arrived with Thomas van Straubenzee as an escort.

Two days later, she and William flew to Klosters for a skiing trip. This time they ignored the five-star Hotel Walserhof and rented an isolated apartment, where Prince Charles joined them later in the week.

April was a month of contrasting emotions for William. The Diana inquest finally came to an end on the seventh, ten-and-a-half years after his mother's death. A jury decided that Diana was unlawfully killed by the "gross negligence" of the paparazzi who had chased the car carrying the princess and Dodi Al Fayed, and by the driver Henri Paul who had been drinking. In a statement issued on the same day as the verdict was announced, William and Harry thanked the jury for the "thorough way in which they have considered the evidence." They added: "We agree with their verdicts."

At times the princes were appalled at details of the role played by the photographers on the night in question. Undoubtedly it has coloured their attitude to the press. When Harry was forced to return from Afghanistan after details of his deployment had been leaked in the press, he arrived back barely able to conceal his anger from the waiting media. Similarly, William has tried his best over the years to ensure that Catherine never has to go through the same sort of pressure from photographers with which his mother had to cope.

During the spring and summer of 2008, Catherine attended four high-profile events in relatively quick succession that left no one in doubt that her position as royal girlfriend was definitely that of a princess-in-waiting.

On 11 April she made her first appearance at a royal engagement since William's Sandhurst graduation 16 months earlier. On that occasion she hadn't been photographed together with the prince. Now she was filmed walking through RAF Cranwell side by side with him. It was presumed that she would attend the event, although her name was not on any official operations notes beforehand.

She watched William and 25 other newly qualified pilots receive their "wings" from the Prince of Wales before she joined the two princes and the Duchess of Cornwall for a private reception with the other graduates and senior staff.

After William successfully completed his intensive flying course, his instructor, Wing Commander Andy Lowell said, "William was very good. I was very impressed by his flying skills. He had a natural ability and was quick to learn."

Unfortunately the kudos earned by the prince for his enthusiasm and commitment was offset when it was leaked that his flight training exercises in a Chinook helicopter involved flights to the family home, Highgrove, and to Sandringham, the Queen's Norfolk estate, as well as landing in the grounds of the Middletons' family home in Berkshire. Although these were justified by the MoD in turn as "a general handling exercise", "low-level flying training" and "practising take-off and landing skills", it was hard not to see them as mere jollies. Worse was to come when it was revealed that the prince had used the Chinook to attend a wedding in Northumberland and, after picking up Harry on the way, also took the chopper to the Isle of Wight for their cousin Peter Phillips' stag party.

Peter's wedding a month later, on 17 May, was Catherine's second high-profile event. Nearly all the royal family were present at St George's Chapel, Windsor, although one significant absentee was William who honoured a long-standing commitment to attend the wedding in Kenya of Batian Craig, Jecca's brother, to Melissa Duveen. The prince's gesture proved how very close he had remained to the Craigs and was in part to thank them for the many holidays he had enjoyed with them, enabling him to escape from the press and public scrutiny in the family's wildlife reserve in the foothills of Mount Kenya.

Another month on, and Catherine was present, again at St George's Chapel, to watch the procession of garter knights walk from the state apartments of Windsor Castle and through the Lower Ward to the chapel. The Order of the Garter is Britain's oldest order of chivalry and William was greatly touched that his grandmother had made him the 1,000th knight.

His grandfather once said of this event, "It's a nice piece of pageantry which I think a lot of people enjoy. Rationally it's lunatic but, in practice, everyone enjoys

ABOVE: *A solemn-looking Catherine leaves her London flat in July 2007 on her way to work at Jigsaw; at the time she and William were not together.*

it, I think." William looked self-conscious in his velvet robes and ostrich-plumed hat as he processed past his girlfriend who was watching from the Galilee Porch. Prince Harry, roaring with laughter, stood next to her, clearly relishing his brother's acute embarrassment.

Catherine's fourth royal event was another wedding. Lady Rose Windsor, the 28-year-old daughter of the Queen's cousin, the Duke of Gloucester, married George Gilman at the Queen's Chapel, next to St James's Palace on 19 July. Catherine looked cool and elegant in a light-blue jacket complementing her multi-coloured silk skirt. In her long flowing hair she wore a black fascinator, that mainstay of modern royal headgear. For once the fashion editors were not concentrating on Miss Middleton but on William's aunt, the Princess Royal, who at 57 arrived wearing the same outfit she wore at Charles and Diana's wedding when she was 31, an abject lesson in royal frugality.

Once again William was absent, this time on board HMS *Iron Duke* on patrol in the Caribbean, as a part of his five-week placement with the Royal Navy. His short stint turned into a bit of a *Boy's Own* adventure. He helped plan exercises to assess the Navy's preparedness should a category five storm hit the volcanic island of Montserrat. Even more exciting was Sub Lt Wales's involvement in a drugs bust when *Iron Duke*, working with the US Coast Guard, seized 45 bales of cocaine valued at £40 million from a speedboat, north-east of Barbados.

Afterwards the ship's captain, Cdr Mark Newland, praised William's maturity and contribution during the seizure, saying "He is a very professional military officer, and very astute".

It had been speculated that William would leave the armed forces in 2009 to become a full-time working royal. In September 2008, Clarence House issued a surprise announcement that the prince intended to train with the RAF Search and Rescue. The course would last 18 months and, if he successfully qualified, he would be committed to serve a unit for three years. The prince's office was keen to point out that he would also still work for the charities and organizations with which he was involved and that he would also undertake some royal duties.

The prince himself said that part of the reason for this change of direction was the fact that, unlike his brother, he was not allowed to serve on the front line: "I now want to build on the experience and training I have received to serve operationally – especially because, for good reasons, I was not able to deploy to Afghanistan this year with D Squadron of the Household Cavalry Regiment."

William was committing himself to the RAF until 2013 and what, queried royal commentators, would that mean about that other pressing commitment – his wedding to Catherine?

While the prince's future was being mapped out, there was still no sign of his girlfriend pursuing a long-term, challenging career. She had quit her job as an accessories buyer for fashion chain Jigsaw in November 2007 after working there for less than a year. The job had been created especially for her by owners

ABOVE: *William amd Instructor Craig Finch at RAF Shrewsbury on 18 June 2009.*

LEFT: *William towers over his father at an RAF wings Graduation Ceremony in April 2008 – at 6 ft 3 in William would be the tallest-ever British monarch.*

John and Belle Robinson and it allowed her the flexibility to maintain her relationship with William.

Belle Robinson found her very unassuming and admired her attitude to the other staff, which she found quite relaxed: "She sat in the kitchen at lunchtime and chatted with everyone from the van drivers to the accounts girls. She wasn't precious."

The Queen, 85 in April 2011, still undertakes almost 400 engagements a year and was reportedly concerned that Catherine was giving herself a work-shy image.

Catherine has been involved with one or two charity ventures. In September 2008, she helped to organize a charity roller disco at the Renaissance Rooms in Vauxhall, in aid of Tom's Ward at Oxford's Children's Hospital. The Middleton sisters were happy to join in the fun. Catherine wore yellow hot pants and a green sparkly top, and at one point was photographed flat on her back, laughing her head off, which set Sarah Ferguson-type alarm bells ringing at the palace.

William's own charity venture was a 1,000-mile bike trip across South Africa which he undertook with Harry. In all, 80 riders took part and the aim was to raise £250,000 for Unicef, the Nelson Mandela Children's Fund and Harry's charity Sentebale. In an eve-of-trip interview Harry said, "We never really spend any time together – we've got separate jobs going on at the moment.

"But it's great fun – well I don't know yet, we'll have to tell you. We might argue, we might have a bit of fun." Prince William joked, "The pain of spending a week with my brother is well worth it."

After the usual Christmas apart, William and Catherine were reunited at Birkhall for a New Year holiday. By now Catherine was working for the family business, Party Pieces. She was reportedly training in website design and launching a new promotion called First Birthdays. It helped to offset some of the criticism that she wasn't the highest of achievers, career-wise, and more importantly it gave her time off whenever William was free to meet her.

William began his training at RAF Shawbury, in Shropshire, on 11 January 2009, two days after he enjoyed a birthday dinner and farewell party rolled into one at the Middletons' home. The same month it was announced that William and Harry would be setting up their own offices in St James's Palace, headed by their private secretary, Jamie Lowther-Pinkerton, a former SAS officer, who had also been an equerry to the Queen Mother in the early 1980s.

In May, Harry also arrived at Shawbury where he started his training as an Army air helicopter pilot. The two brothers shared a rented cottage and in a joint interview they talked about the novelty of sharing a home and tackling housework – with William claiming he was the one in charge. "Bearing in mind I cook, I feed him [Harry] every day, I think he's done very well," he said.

"Harry does do washing up but then he leaves most of it in the sink and then I come back in the morning and I have to wash it up." William continued, "I do a fair bit of tidying up after him. He snores a lot, too."

ABOVE: *During their trip to the child education centre William and Harry delight the children by playing a game of football with them.*

At this point Harry joked, "Oh God, they'll think we share a bed now. We're brothers not lovers!" As Harry explained it would be the "first time, last time we'll live together", William added dryly, "It's been an emotional experience."

The sightings of William and Catherine were getting fewer and fewer. In May 2009, they met up when William was on leave and attended a charity polo match at Coworth Park near Ascot. They had spent the previous night at his private apartment at Clarence House, where Catherine had asked him to install a basic gym, so she could keep toned without having to go to a health club.

During the same leave, William made a private visit to meet 109-year-old Catherine Masters at the Grange Care Centre in Standford in the Vale, Oxfordshire. Earlier in the year, Mrs Masters had contacted Buckingham Palace to complain that her annual birthday card from the Queen was always the same design. Having accrued quite a stack of them over the years, she was tired of seeing Her Majesty in the same canary yellow dress. William apologized and promised to ensure his grandmother was wearing a different outfit next year.

Later in the summer, the prince was photographed kissing Catherine in the car park of The Potting Shed, in the village of Crudwell, a popular watering hole with the Cotswold polo playing set.

It was to stop such snatched photos appearing that prompted an authorized crackdown on the paparazzi in the run-up to the traditional Christmas break at Sandringham. A statement released on 5 December said that members of the royal family would now be prepared to take legal action against what they see as the "intrusive and unacceptable behaviour" of photographers. The crackdown once again fuelled rumours that a royal engagement was in the offing, and the media crossed its collective fingers and waited.

Eventually, 2010 would finally provide the royal news that so many people had begun to suspect would never happen.

ENGAGEMENT

William and Catherine spent Christmas 2009 apart, as royal partners only receive an invitation to join the festivities at Sandringham after they are engaged. Shortly before 11 o'clock on Christmas Day, William walked through the snow-laden paths of the Queen's Norfolk estate to attend matins at the tiny church of St Mary Magdalene. Catherine meanwhile enjoyed a family Christmas with her parents, sister and brother in Bucklebury, Berkshire.

LEFT: *The prince and his fiancée exchange loving, happy glances as they pose for the press on the occasion of the public announcement of their engagement on 16 November 2010.*

They met up for New Year at Birkhall and again two weeks later when William successfully completed his advanced helicopter-training course. He was presented with his certificate by his father at a ceremony at RAF Shawbury on 15 January. Catherine was in the audience and rose to her feet and applauded enthusiastically when the prince's name was announced.

In the past, William had often looked tense when Catherine was present, perhaps sensing that they were the focus of attention and a distraction, whether they were at a royal ceremony or attending a friend's wedding. Throughout 2010 they threw caution to the wind and appeared relaxed and happy on the few occasions they were seen together. At Shawbury, for instance, Catherine sat next to the prince throughout the ceremony, their body language less tense, as they smiled broadly and whispered to each other.

In his speech, Prince Charles spoke about the dangers facing a search and rescue pilot as well as poking fun at some of the less onerous tasks: "Some of you no doubt will find yourselves in Afghanistan where the ground troops will put great faith in you.

"Others no doubt among you will be plucking people from danger, maybe sheep in distress, not to mention endless ladies with conveniently sprained ankles on awkward mountainsides across the country."

Later in the month Flight Lieutenant Wales arrived at RAF Anglesey to start his training, hoping to become a fully operational pilot by the summer, having learned the skills required to operate Sea King helicopters.

The prince also took another important step forward in his apprenticeship as monarch when he represented the Queen at the opening of the new £38-million Supreme Court in Wellington during a five-day visit to New Zealand. It was to be his first official overseas trip and he told officials it meant "an awful lot" to him. During his tour he showed he was imbued with the qualities of both his parents. His visit to the wildlife reserve of Kapiti Island off the north island's western coast, a haven for rare birds, mirrored the environmental concerns of his father. Earlier, his easy relationship with members of the public on a walkabout in Wellington evoked memories of Diana's people skills.

When Meryl Best, 41, told him she had been "privileged" to meet Diana on her visit to Christchurch in 1983, the prince asked: "What was she doing?" "She was looking beautiful," came the reply. William responded, "She did that elegantly," and then, after shaking more hands, he turned to Mrs Best a second time and said gratefully, "You are a very special lady. I will shake your hand again."

A month later, the prince charmed another crowd, this time a homegrown one, outside London's Royal Opera House, when he made his first appearance at the British Academy Film Awards. The 27-year-old royal received some of the loudest screams of the A-list celebrity-packed night, with girls clamouring to kiss him and to be photographed with him.

RIGHT: *Although they actually got engaged in October 2010, Catherine and Prince William chose 16 November to announce the news to the world. The 2011 wedding was set to be the largest royal event since the prince's parents, Prince Charles and Lady Diana, were married on 29 July 1981.*

FOLLOWING PAGES: *Royal grandeur: the world's press gather for a photocall in the State Rooms of St James's Palace as Prince William and Catherine Middleton announce their engagement in November 2010.*

Dressed in a dinner suit, the prince walked on stage with the Hollywood star Uma Thurman to present a BAFTA fellowship to legendary actress Vanessa Redgrave. Despite being an avowed republican, Ms Redgrave bowed down on bended knee and was beaming as William helped her back to her feet and kissed her on both cheeks.

In June, William and Harry travelled to Africa to carry out their first official joint overseas engagements, visiting Botswana, Lesotho and South Africa on behalf of three charities: Tusk Trust, Sentebale and the Football Association. Sentebale was jointly founded by Harry and Prince Seeiso of Lesotho and the latter joined the two brothers as they rode on horseback to visit schools and orphanages in the country's snow-capped mountains. They wore grey knitted blankets like those worn by local Basotho herdsmen. The children had embroidered "Prince William Arthur Philip Louis" on his, while his brother's had the touching message "Thank You Harry".

William's next visit to Africa was a Kenyan safari with Catherine in October 2010 and, as we discovered in due course, it was to be a pretty unforgettable holiday since it was here that he proposed to the woman who had been by his friend and companion for eight years. Later William would only reveal the exact location was "somewhere nice in Kenya" – pretty much an understatement as it was in Mount Kenya National Park, at one of the lakes on the side of the mountain.

The prince hired a helicopter to take him and Catherine to Lake Rutundu and Lake Alice, which are surrounded by snowy peaks and forests of heather. They flew from the Lewa Downs safari lodge in which he and Catherine had stayed with Jecca Craig's family five years earlier. He had been carrying his mother's sapphire-and-diamond engagement ring in his rucksack and, in this most sublime of settings, produced it to an unsuspecting Catherine and asked her to be his wife.

There are strong links between the royal family and Kenya. It was against this same backdrop that William's grandmother became Queen at the tender age of 25 when her father died suddenly in his sleep, while she and Prince Philip were on tour, staying at Treetops Hotel in Aberdare National Park.

William had spent part of his gap year working in North Kenya and later said, "It was the happiest time of my life," as none of his companions on anti-poaching patrols knew about his background and for once he could enjoy a period of anonymity.

Back home again, the question now was how to keep the news a secret until the official announcement. The couple had one joint public appearance to make on 24 October at the wedding of their friends Harry Meade and Rosie Bradford in Northleach, Gloucestershire.

It was the first time Catherine had been seen since attending polo at the Beaufort Club on 10 July. She looked stunning in an electric-blue silk dress with

ABOVE: *Catherine's engagement ring is that worn by William's mother when she got engaged to Prince Charles. William said that giving Catherine the ring – a dazzling oval blue 18-carat sapphire and diamond piece – was his way of ensuring that his late mother was involved in the occasion.*

LEFT: *In Bucklebury, Berkshire, Michael and Carole Middleton deliver a statement outside their home following the news of the engagement; the parents of the bride-to-be said they were "absolutely delighted" at the news.*

FOLLOWING PAGES: *The Middletons' home in Bucklebury was besieged with photographers as soon as the engagement was announced, and a police guard became the norm.*

a black jacket and hat. In the past they had nearly always arrived separately to avoid being photographed together and so royal commentators interpreted the couple's arrival side by side as "very unusual and very significant". "Will they be next?" queried one headline. Rumours abounded that they had already got engaged while on a trip to Balmoral, which Clarence House could legitimately dismiss as "categorically untrue".

The death of Catherine's grandfather Peter Middleton on 2 November delayed the official announcement. Eventually it came on Tuesday 16 November, and although it had been anticipated for years, it seemed like a bolt out of the blue, as everyone had become accustomed to the status quo.

A statement from Clarence House proclaimed that the "Prince of Wales is delighted to announce the engagement of Prince William to Miss Catherine Middleton". In tune with the modern age, the news was posted on the Queen's Facebook page and as a "tweet" on the royal Twitter site, as well as notification by the old-fashioned e-mail method.

After a massive press call at St James's Palace at 4.45 pm, in which the couple posed amid a blitz of flash bulbs, they pre-recorded an interview with Tom Bradby, ITV's political editor and former royal correspondent. William's press secretary, Miguel Head, in a press note to media organizations, said, "The couple

asked to record this interview specifically with Mr Bradby, whom they have both known for some time."

William admitted, "We had been talking about marriage for a while, so it wasn't a massively big surprise. I'd been planning it for a while, but as any guy out there will know, it takes a certain amount of motivation to get yourself going." He revealed that he took so long to propose because he wanted Catherine to have the chance to "back out" if she felt that she could not cope with life as a future queen.

Although the public are familiar with Catherine's features, few outside the magic royal circle had ever heard her speak and, given that she must have been nervous, she was surprisingly articulate in the interview and spoke with a well-modulated tone. Recalling the proposal, she laughed as she said, "It was very romantic. There's a true romantic in there." She also revealed that the proposal had been as much of a surprise to her as it was to the rest of us. "Because we were out with friends and things, so I really didn't expect it all. I thought he might have maybe thought about it but no. It was a total shock when it came."

William talked candidly about his mother. Her sapphire-and-diamond ring "is very special to me", he said. "As Catherine's very special to me now, it was right to put the two together." Referring poignantly to Diana, he added, "Because obviously she's not going to be around to share any of the fun and excitement of it all – this was my way of keeping her close to it all."

The prince was asked if he'd sought Michael Middleton's permission. "Well, I was torn between asking Catherine's dad first and then the realization that he might actually say 'no' dawned upon me. So I thought if I ask Catherine first then he can't really say no. So I did it that way round. I managed to speak to Mike soon after it happened really and then it sort of happened from there."

Catherine added that her mother was "absolutely over the moon". She also said, "And actually we had quite an awkward situation because I knew that William had asked my father but I didn't know if my mother knew. So I came back from Scotland and my mother didn't make it clear to me whether she knew or not, so both of us were there sort of looking at each other and feeling quite awkward about it. But it was amazing to tell her and obviously she was very happy for us."

Referring to her family as "important to me", Catherine added, "I hope we will be able to have a happy family ourselves," while William joked, "I think we'll take it one step at a time. We'll sort of get over the marriage first and then maybe look at the kids. But obviously we want a family so we'll have to start thinking about that."

At one point Catherine admitted, "It's obviously nerve-wracking, because I don't know the ropes really." William was more relaxed and jokey about the stress: "We're like sort of ducks, very calm on the surface with little feet going

RIGHT: *The day after the royal engagement was announced, the British press made a big splash of the news across its front pages.*

under the water. It's been really exciting. We've been talking about it for a long time, so for us it's a real relief and it's really nice to be able to tell everybody."

News of the royal romance was immediately flashed around the world, with major overseas news stations such as ABC's *Good Morning America* opening their bulletin with a trumpeted fanfare over photos of the couple. In Britain, Prime Minister David Cameron said the engagement marked "a great day for Britain". The Queen said she was "absolutely delighted" for them, while Prince Charles concurred, and joked that "they have been practising long enough". Speaking from his Berkshire home, Michael Middleton said, "We have got to know William really well. We all think he is wonderful and we are extremely fond of him. They make a lovely couple."

Perhaps the most touching comment came from the man who for so long has been William's best friend, and will soon be Catherine's brother-in-law, Prince Harry, who said, "I'm delighted that my brother has popped the question. It means I get a sister, which I have always wanted."

ABOVE: *RAF Valley – with its welcome sign in English and Welsh – is many miles away from London's boutiques and bars. However, the couple were said to relish the potential for privacy afforded by rural North Wales.*

RIGHT: *On their first public appearance together after announcing their engagement, William and Catherine attended a Teenage Cancer Trust charity fundraising gala in Thursford, Norfolk in December 2010.*

THE WEDDING

An estimated two billion people watched the royal wedding on TVs, mobile phones, laptops, YouTube and on every other conceivable form of modern broadcasting media. Five thousand street parties took place throughout the UK and one million people packed the processional route from Buckingham Palace to Westminster Abbey. Film crews came from as far afield as Brazil and the Ukraine and photographers paid up to £1,000 for the prime spot opposite the palace balcony to capture that much-anticipated kiss.

LEFT: *The future King William V and Queen Catherine pose with their families in the Throne Room at Buckingham Palace for a formal wedding photograph. Front row (L-R): Grace van Cutsem, Eliza Lopes (Camilla's granddaughter), Prince Philip Duke of Edinburgh, Queen Elizabeth II, Margarita Armstrong-Jones (the Queen's great niece), Lady Louise Windsor (daughter of Prince Edward) and William Lowther-Pinkerton. Back Row (L-R): Tom Pettifer, Camilla Duchess of Cornwall, Prince Charles, Prince Harry, Michael Middleton, Carole Middleton, James Middleton and Philippa Middleton.*

Why was the wedding of William Arthur Philip Louis Windsor to Catherine Elizabeth Middleton such a global phenomenon? The most obvious answer is that it had it all. It had the magnetic combination of royalty, style, glamour, pageantry and, perhaps most important of all, it was clearly a love match.

William's parents only dated each other for a year or so before 20-year-old Lady Diana Spencer made that terrifying walk down the nave of St Paul's Cathedral, "like a lamb to slaughter", as she told biographer Andrew Morton. Prince Andrew and Sarah Ferguson were also romantically linked for just a year before their Abbey wedding in 1986, as had Princess Anne and Mark Phillips been a decade earlier. All three marriages ended in 1992 – the year described by the Queen as an "annus horribilis" – when Anne was divorced and it was announced that Andrew and "Fergie" and then Charles and Diana were to separate.

PREVIOUS PAGE: *Catherine prepares to enter the Abbey with her sister Pippa holding her train. Pippa's elegant white dress was designed by Sarah Burton for Alexander McQueen.*

LEFT: *Michael Middleton leads his daughter Catherine down the aisle, followed by her attendants. The choir sing Parry's "I Was Glad" as they pass.*

BELOW: *Prince William takes Catherine's right hand and places a wedding ring made of traditional Welsh gold on her fourth finger.*

By the time William and Catherine met at the very beginning of the 21st century, the House of Windsor was beginning to change. Precedent and protocol were ignored and royal couples were allowed to get to know each other well and were not steamrollered into marriage. It began when Prince Edward met public-relations worker Sophie Rhys-Jones in 1993. Edward and Sophie were a couple for a full six years before they married in June 1999. The last royal bride of the 20th century had been fully schooled in all aspects of life with the Windsors at the same time as she was slowly getting to know her husband-to-be in the way any other woman would.

William and Catherine's romance was even more slow-burning than his uncle and aunt's. They split up twice, first as students at St Andrews University and then again in the spring of 2007 when William felt trapped. Free to go his own way, the prince

PREVIOUS PAGES: *A bird's-eye views shows the couple kneeling at the high altar for the closing prayers.*

LEFT: *William leads his wife out of the Edward the Confessor Chapel after the signing of the register.*

BELOW: *Catherine looking relaxed as she greets guests at a lunchtime reception hosted by the Queen at Buckingham Palace following the wedding. Here she chats to the Governor-General of Canada, His Excellency the Rt Hon David Johnston, and Mrs Sharon Johnston.*

ABOVE: *In a surprise break with tradition, William borrowed his father's beloved open-topped Aston Martin for the short drive from Buckingham Palace to Clarence House. William had changed into a Blues and Royals captain's frock coat, but Catherine delighted the crowds by remaining in her wedding dress.*

discovered that life on the nightclub circuit, while undoubtedly fun, was not the way he was going to meet a future wife with the qualities of a queen consort.

Back together again by August of the same year, the couple re-established a low-key romantic life away from the fast lane and the ever-present paparazzi. Life for them then, and now, is a world away from that led by Charles and Diana. Instead, they are as near to an ordinary couple as their position allows – content to eat pizza in front of the TV in their Anglesey hideaway rather than join the A-list circuit in London.

This combination of the ordinary and the extraordinary seems to fascinate people. We know that William and Catherine are clearly the best of friends, university mates who have clicked, like so many of their St Andrews contemporaries did. Yet we also know that one day they will succeed to the British throne – and whatever Commonwealth realms still survive – as King William V and Queen Catherine.

It was this mixture of the ordinary and extraordinary – the private and the public – that was so evident at the royal wedding. There were the traditional hymns, the Archbishop of Canterbury conducting the ceremony, the curtsey to the Queen, the RAF flypast and the 1902 State Landau – the same carriage used by William's parents – for the return journey. But there was also the new, the innovative and the very personal side to this wedding. The couple prepared their own prayer in which they thanked God "for our families, for the love that we share and for the joy of our marriage". They also asked the Almighty to "keep our eyes fixed on what is real and important in life" and to "help us to serve and comfort those who suffer".

The innovative side was most obvious in aspects of the décor of the ceremony. Under other circumstances Catherine Middleton would have married near her family home at Bucklebury in Berkshire. Bucklebury Common is famous for its Avenue of Oaks at Chapel Row and in Westminster Abbey eight 6-metre- (20-foot-) high trees – six maple and two hornbeam – replicated that avenue, bringing rural England into the heart of London.

The wedding reception was similarly more personal than the "wedding breakfast" that palace staff traditionally create for the royal party and their closest friends. For the weddings of the Queen and Queen Mother, for instance, only a small fraction of the guests could attend the sit-down meal. William and Kate opted for a more relaxed, buffet-style reception hosted by the Queen for

BELOW: *Prince Harry decorated his father's car with balloons, ribbons and this distinctive number plate for his brother and sister-in-law.*

LEFT: *On the evening of the wedding, Catherine prepares to leave Clarence House for a private dinner party for 300 close friends and family. The new Duchess of Cambridge had changed into a flowing white satin gown, accessorized with a diamante detail at the waist and an angora bolero cardigan. Like her wedding dress, it was designed by Sarah Burton for Alexander McQueen.*

around 650 guests.

That's not to say the reception wasn't lavish. Mark Flanagan, the royal chef, aided by a team of 21 other chefs, prepared 10,000 mouthwatering canapés. Guests were served, among other things, Pressed Duck Terrine with Fruit Chutney, Smoked Scottish Salmon Rose on Beetroot Blini, Langoustines with Lemon Mayonnaise, Pressed Confit of Pork Belly and Bubble and Squeak with Confit Shoulder of Lamb. This feast was washed down with Pol Roger Non-Vintage Brut Réserve Champagne as well as a selection of other soft and alcoholic drinks.

Instead of being trapped at a top table in the palace ballroom, William and Catherine were free to wander through the State Apartments to talk to friends and relatives, while in the background Claire Jones, the official harpist to the Prince of Wales, provided subtle ambient music.

The couple cut the official wedding cake designed by Fiona Cairns. Made from 17 individual fruit cakes, 12 of which formed the base, it had eight tiers and was decorated in cream and white icing. Cairns added 900 individual flowers including the English rose, Scottish thistle, Welsh daffodil and Irish shamrock. Again, with that mixture of formal and informal that characterized

ABOVE: *After spending their first night as man and wife at Buckingham Palace, the next morning the couple walk hand-in-hand to a waiting helicopter as they leave for a secret honeymoon location.*

this wedding, the couple also cut a chocolate biscuit cake – William's favourite – created for the prince by McVitie's from a royal family recipe.

After the reception ended at 3.35pm, William drove his new bride the short distance from Buckingham Palace to Clarence House. In another personal touch, Prince Charles had allowed his son to drive his beloved two-seater Aston Martin BD6 which was decorated with balloons by Prince Harry and given the rear number plate "JU5T WED" for the day. A few months later it emerged that William caused his father to wince by roaring off with the handbrake still on.

The groom had changed into the frock coat of a Blues and Royals captain but Catherine still wore her wedding dress, to the delight of the crowd who had a second chance to see it. Overhead a yellow Sea King helicopter flying the RAF ensign dipped in salute to the couple – a surprise organized by RAF Wattisham to honour the UK's most famous search and rescue pilot.

Later the couple returned to Buckingham Palace to attend an evening reception hosted by Prince Charles. The Queen had by now left to allow the younger generation to relax at a less formal party for close friends and the younger royals.

Catherine wore an evening dress designed by Sarah Burton who had also created her wedding dress. It was a strapless white dress with a fitted bodice and an embroidered waistband. Over her shoulders she wore an elegant shrug to keep off the slight chill of a late spring evening. After dinner the couple partied until the small hours. Singer-songwriter Ellie Goulding performed at the event and her cover version of the Elton John classic "Your Song" was William and Catherine's first dance. The evening ended at 3am with a small fireworks display in the palace grounds.

Having spent their first night as man and wife in Buckingham Palace, the following morning the couple left by helicopter for what was described by a spokesperson for Prince William as "a private destination". In contrast to the day before, when a million onlookers cheered them on the way to the Abbey, only two footmen were on hand to say goodbye to William and Catherine as they emerged hand-in-hand from the palace and strolled to the helicopter in bright sunshine. For this most private of public couples it was just the sort of restrained departure they had wanted.

Later in the year Catherine's wedding dress was again centre stage when it was announced it would be the star attraction of the annual summer opening of the Buckingham Palace State Apartments. Before the exhibition was opened to the public there was a private viewing for two VIP guests, Queen Elizabeth II and the bride herself, the future Queen Catherine.

Something about the ghost-like appearance of the headless mannequin used to exhibit the gown seemed to upset the Queen, who was overheard by film crew to describe it as "horrible", adding, "It's made to look very creepy." Catherine bravely chipped in with her own opinion, saying it had a "3D effect". For once the public disagreed with the monarch. By the end of the day on which it was announced that the wedding dress was to be exhibited, a spokesman for the Royal Collection said, "It's incredible, the phones have been in melt-down for advance tickets."

Wedding fever proved hard to shake off and a new expression – "the Kate effect" – was linked to everything from British fashion to the sale of souvenirs.

LEFT, TOP: *Tourists queue outside Buckingham Palace as it opens to the public on 23 July 2011 for the summer exhibition, at which the star attraction was the royal wedding dress.*

LEFT, BOTTOM: *The famous dress, complete with its veil and tiara and 2.7-metre (nine-foot) train, displayed on a raised oval stage.*

ABOVE: *The Queen and Catherine pay a private visit to see the dress and other wedding memorabilia on 22 July 2011, the day before the exhibition opened to the public. It appeared the mannequin's lack of a head may have perturbed the Queen.*

CANADA &
THE USA

It was back in early February 2011, ten weeks before the royal wedding and with only one joint public engagement under their belt, that it was announced that William and Catherine would visit Canada in June of that year. If the decision to launch the Duchess onto the world's stage so soon after the wedding was a surprise, the choice of Canada was far less surprising.

LEFT: *William and Catherine join in Canada Day celebrations at Parliament Hill, Ottawa, on 1 July 2011. The Duchess's choice of a hat and coat to match the Canadian flag shows she's already mastered the art of fashion diplomacy.*

William and Catherine began their tour on 30 June. Catherine had boarded the plane wearing a navy-blue dress called "Manon" by French designer Roland Mouret, teamed with a navy blazer by Canadian fashion house Smythe Les Vestes. This was serious sartorial flattery and there was more to follow: for their arrival, she changed into a navy lace dress by Montreal-born Erdem Moralioglu.

Even before any official welcome, the couple laid a wreath at the Tomb of the Unknown Soldier at Canada's National War Memorial. The next day was Canada Day: Catherine wore a white Reiss dress and a red maple-leaf hat, to the delight of the 300,000-strong crowd in Ottawa She also wore a diamond maple-leaf brooch that had been presented to the Queen Mother on her first Canadian tour in 1939.

In William's first speech, he spoke French, Canada's second official language. What he lacked in linguistic skill he made up for in enthusiasm, breaking off to say in English: "Don't worry, it'll improve…" The start of his second speech was more rock star than royalty: "*Bonjour* Ottawa! *Bonjour* Canada! *Bonne fête* Canada!" He went on: "I'm excited to be able to share this with Catherine,

BELOW: *Deep in concentration, William and Catherine seem oblivious to the surrounding press and dignitaries as they visit a children's cancer ward at Sainte-Justine University Hospital in Montreal on 2 July 2011.*

RIGHT: *Catherine used to play hockey at school and is only too happy to throw the puck for this game at Somba K'e Civic Plaza, Yellowknife. William joined in one of the games but Catherine's beige Malene Birger dress and nude LK Bennett shoes weren't very practical for a rough-and-tumble match.*

RIGHT, BELOW: *The couple were able to take a break alone on Eagle Island on Blachford Lake, in the Northwest Territory. Guiding them is Francois Paulette (in the stern of the canoe), who took them to a private lodge for a few hours.*

because she [...] heard about Canada [...] from her grandfather, a wonderful man who passed away last year, but who held this country dear to his heart – for he trained in Alberta as a young pilot during the Second World War." He also passed on the Queen's "warmest good wishes to the people of Canada".

Next came the province of Quebec, where they visited Sainte-Justine Hospital in Montreal, then joined a cookery workshop. William created a herb-and-cranberry-crusted lamb confit and lobster soufflé while Catherine produced hors d'oeuvres.

On Prince Edward Island, William flew a Sea King helicopter, practising the emergency-landing manoeuvre "waterbirding" while Catherine photographed. Later they competed in a dragon-boat race. They then moved on to Yellowknife, Northwest Territories, land of the midnight sun, meeting aboriginal groups.

On day seven, instead of taking a day off as scheduled, William and Catherine visited Slave Lake in Alberta which had been ravaged by wildfire six weeks before, destroying 400 households. They met those affected and walked around the town.

An overnight stay at secluded Skoki Lodge in Banff National Park gave them a brief taste of life in the Rockies. They also enjoyed a quiet trip on Blanchford Lake, with a dinner of caribou steak and whitefish cooked on an open fire.

On their final night in Canada, William made a touching speech in which he revealed they had both fallen in love with this country. "In 1939, my great-grandmother, Queen Elizabeth the Queen Mother, said of her first tour of Canada

PREVIOUS PAGES, LEFT: *Catherine again wears Canada red with the Queen's diamond Maple Leaf Brooch to wave farewell at Calgary airport on 8 July. William said: "Our promise to Canada is that we shall return."*

PREVIOUS PAGES, RIGHT: *Two of the world's most famous women meet. Catherine talks to US First Lady Michelle Obama during a private meeting at Buckingham Palace on 24 May 2011.*

ABOVE: *In California, Catherine poses with William's victorious polo team after presenting their cup. The event was in aid of the American Friends of the Foundation of Prince William and Prince Harry, which supports disadvantaged children, conservation causes and military veterans and their families.*

RIGHT: *After the match Catherine presented each competitor with a blue Tiffany & Co box with a white ribbon, and her husband with a kiss.*

with her husband King George VI, 'Canada made us'. Catherine and I now know very well what she meant. Canada has far surpassed all that we were promised."

On 9 July, the couple flew to Los Angeles. Catherine, wearing a lavender Peridot dress by Serbian-born Roksanda Illinic, was handed a red, white and blue bouquet to echo the UK and US flags; it was her first visit to the US. They were there for a UK Trade and Investment-sponsored meeting to promote British technological business, at the Beverley Hilton where 200 screaming fans greeted them.

The couple stayed at the British Consul's residence in Haydock Park, attending a garden party with LA's finest, including former England footballer David Beckham and head of Disney Bob Iger. Once again Kate made a diplomatic fashion choice, appearing in a "Maja" green silk dress by American couturier Diane Von Furstenberg, with a bag by the same designer.

Next they went to Santa Barbara for a charity polo match. Celebrities paid up to $4,000 a ticket to attend and $60,000 to play in the match. The event raised over $5 million for charity. Catherine, dressed in a silver and marble-grey hand-painted

BELOW: *William, as President of the British Academy of Film and Television Arts, attended the 2011 BAFTA "Brits to Watch" event at the Belasco Theater on 9 July 2011. Catherine looks effortlessly stylish in an Alexander McQueen gown and diamond earrings loaned to her by Queen Elizabeth.*

chinoiserie silk dress by Jenny Packham, delighted guests and photographers by presenting a trophy to her husband and kissing him on both cheeks.

The highlight of the US visit was a dinner hosted by the British Academy of Film and Television Arts in LA. William introduced film-studio executives to 42 "Brits to Watch": up-and-coming UK actors, producers and animators. In a speech, he asked: "Please give them the opportunities you have always extended to some of the brightest and best that Britain has to offer. When American and British creative talent gets together magic happens." Among the 42 was actress Jessica Brown-Findlay, Lady Sybil Crawley in ITV's *Downton Abbey*, who discovered that the royal couple are fans of the costume drama.

Hollywood's finest, among them Nicole Kidman, Barbra Streisand and Jennifer Lopez, paid $25,000 per table to break bread with the royals. Actor Jason Bateman told reporters: "They are the ultimate movie stars. We're all just kind of faking it and getting paid for it. They are the real deal."

On the final morning, the couple attended a reception for US patrons of Tusk Trust, a conservation charity supported by William. They also visited Inner City Arts, a performance-art centre for deprived youths. Their last point of call was the "Hiring Our Heroes" job fair for returning troops. Kelly York, a 23-year-old Air Force veteran looking for a job, voiced the general reaction: "I'm sure that they had 50 million places they could go and see. The fact that they even take five minutes to stop here and say something to the veterans, that's huge.".

ABOVE: *On the final day of their US visit, the royal couple visited the Inner City Arts Center in Los Angeles and were very much hands-on. Here Catherine laughs as William teases her about the large red snail she painted.*

PRIVATE & PUBLIC WORK

William and Catherine's working life is centred around the office they share with Prince Harry in St James's Palace. In January 2009 the Queen granted her two grandsons a joint Royal Household which, according to a Palace press release, "lays the basis for the princes' lives in the future as they progress their public, military and charitable activities". Since the royal wedding, it has expanded to include Catherine's public role as a member of the royal family.

LEFT: *Catherine presents service medals to members of the Irish Guards at the Victoria Barracks in Windsor on 25 June 2011. The Queen made William a Colonel of the Irish Guards two months before his wedding.*

The head of the Household is Jamie Lowther-Pinkerton, William's most trusted aide. The former SAS officer is distantly related to the princes, all of them being descended from William Ponsonby, 1st Viscount Duncannon, an ancestor of the late Queen Mother, to whom Lowther-Pinkerton was an equerry for the period 1984–86. After that he was handpicked by the then Prime Minister, Margaret Thatcher, to lead two major SAS counter-narcotics operations against the drug lords of Colombia in 1989. Five years later he was part of a specialist SAS operation in Bosnia. Lowther-Pinkerton returned to royal service in March 2005 when Prince Charles interviewed him for the post of Private Secretary. He lives in Suffolk with his wife Susannah and their four children. One of his sons, William, was a pageboy at the royal wedding.

The royal couple's private diary is organized by Helen Asprey, a scion of the jewellery family, who has been William's personal assistant since 2000. Before that she worked in the Duke of Edinburgh's office at Buckingham Palace. She deals with the private correspondence of William, Catherine and Harry as well as co-ordinating their private diaries and overseeing holidays and weekends away.

The staff also includes public relations chief Miguel Head, a former career diplomat on secondment from the Foreign Office, who was largely responsible for the smooth running of the 2011 North American tour. In addition, in 2009 the Queen appointed Sir David Manning, former British Ambassador to the USA, as part-time advisor to the princes and their Household.

At present Catherine doesn't have a lady-in-waiting, essential for any royal lady in the past but now largely ignored in the working lives of Camilla Duchess of Cornwall and Sophie Wessex. On occasions Helen Asprey has stood in as her assistant, notably to visit Westminster Abbey before confirming it as the wedding venue.

In her post-divorce years, Diana occasionally asked her sister Sarah McCorquodale to accompany her on royal engagements, and it is conceivable that Pippa Middleton could accept a similar role in Catherine's life. However, given the media circus that accompanies either sister whenever they appear in public, it is unlikely royal advisors would be happy with Pippa joining the team.

Two royal in-laws have helped ease Catherine's transition to royal life. She is particularly close to William's stepmother Camilla. The two met for lunch in Koffman's restaurant at the Berkeley Hotel in Knightsbridge in the run-up to the wedding, where the Duchess of Cornwall was overheard by a fellow diner saying, "If I can give you one bit of advice…".

That "bit of advice" may well have been for Catherine to try to preserve some of her own identity in her new life. Camilla has kept on her former home, Ray Mill House at Laycock in Wiltshire, as a bolt hole where she can be her old self. She sets aside one day a week to play grandma to her five grandchildren. She also goes on what she calls "bucket and spade" holidays each summer with her children and their families.

ABOVE: *Jamie Lowther-Pinkerton (Prince William and Prince Harry's Private Secretary) attends the annual Chelsea Pensioners Founders' Day Parade on 9 June 2011 at the Royal Hospital, Chelsea, in southwest London.*

William reportedly asked his aunt, Sophie Wessex, to take Catherine under her wing and pass on advice, so that his wife was more prepared for her role than his mother had been. Diana was almost a decade younger than Catherine when she married into the royal family and would later complain that she had been thrown in at the deep end and given little training. Sophie has faced several challenges. Tying to balance royal life with running her own public-relations company led to a conflict of interest, most famously when a potential client turned out to be an undercover reporter. The Countess was recorded making unflattering comments about members of the government as well as her royal relations, and appeared to be abusing her royal status to gain clients. The following year both she and Prince Edward abandoned their careers to concentrate on royal duties. It was a painful but invaluable lesson.

It was no doubt with the lessons of Camilla, Sophie and, particularly, Diana in mind that William and Catherine's public engagements were limited and tightly controlled. Their first royal duty as a married couple was a diplomatic one. On 24 May they met US President Barack Obama and his wife Michelle at Buckingham Palace on the first day of their state visit to the UK. The newlyweds

BELOW: *Soldiers escort Queen Elizabeth II up the Mall following the Trooping the Colour ceremony on 11 June 2011. More than 600 guardsmen and cavalry make up the parade. The Trooping the Colour is believed to have first been performed during the reign of King Charles II. In 1748, it was decided that the parade would be used to mark the official birthday of the sovereign. Queen Elizabeth's actual birthday is on 21 April.*

greeted the Obamas in the opulent 1844 Room, designed for the state visit of Emperor Nicholas I of Russia to Queen Victoria. The meeting took place a few days after William and Catherine returned from their Seychelles honeymoon and they both looked relaxed in their 20 minutes or so with the visitors. It had been widely speculated that one or both of the Obamas would be invited to the royal wedding. This was not, however, a state occasion, so only royalty and Commonwealth leaders were invited. The palace meeting was seen as intended to offset any criticism that the Obamas had been snubbed over the wedding.

On 9 June the Cambridges made their first public appearance as a married couple, at a lavish gala dinner in a pavilion at Kensington Palace, William's childhood home, to mark the tenth anniversary of the Absolute Return for Kids (ARK) charity. They shared a table with 24 other famous faces, including Baron de Rothschild, socialite Jemima Khan, actor Colin Firth, fashion designer Tom Ford and Prince Pavlos of Greece and his wife Marie Chantal. Catherine wore a floor-length rose-pink sequinned organza Jenny Packham evening gown, which retails at £3,835, and matching LK Bennett shoes costing £175. Addressing the audience at the dinner, William said: "My brother, Catherine and I hope to use our philanthropy as a long-term catalyst for meaningful change."

Two days later came Trooping the Colour. The Duchess shared a barouche with Camilla from Buckingham Palace to Horse Guards Parade, where she

ABOVE & RIGHT: *Following Trooping the Colour, the royal family normally gathers on the palace balcony for the traditional flypast to honour the Queen's birthday. Here Catherine and William are joined by the Earl and Countess of Wessex and their daughter Lady Louise Windsor as they watch the spectacular Red Arrows fly over in formation.*

watched her husband arrive on horseback as part of the Queen's escort. Afterwards they appeared on the balcony of Buckingham Palace.

The next week, Catherine was in Windsor Castle to see William take part in the annual Garter Service. In the procession of Garter Knights, he walked ahead of his grandmother from the State Apartments and into the Lower Ward of the castle precincts. Catherine watched with Camilla from the Galilee Porch and made her husband blush as she caught his eye and beamed at him.

Also in Windsor, at Victoria Barracks, Catherine and the prince handed out operational medals to members of the Irish Guards. The soldiers had recently returned from service in Afghanistan. William had been made the regiment's colonel earlier in the year and wore his Irish Guards' uniform at his wedding. He spoke of his "pride and humility" in being there, and a royal aide said the Duchess was pleased to present medals to a regiment "so close to her husband's heart".

On 4 June 2011, William, Catherine and Harry were surprise guests at the

Epsom Derby to cheer on the Queen's horse. In 1953, the year of her coronation, the Queen's horse Aureole came second at the Derby but she had never achieved the ultimate accolade of owning the Derby winner. Finally, in 2011, she had a strong chance: Carlton House was hot favourite. The royal family came out in force to support the Queen, with four of her grandchildren – William, Harry, Beatrice and Eugenie – present, as well as Prince Andrew and the Earl and Countess of Wessex. Sadly Her Majesty's dream was not fulfilled.

With the sun beating down, Catherine looked cool and summery in a floaty white Reiss dress. Known as the Peacock, it, like many of her other high-street buys, sold out almost immediately after she was seen wearing it. She teamed it with a jacket by Joseph, together with nude LK Bennett shoes and a matching clutch bag. It was the Duchess's second Reiss outfit in less than a fortnight, her first being the £175 dress she wore to meet the Obamas.

Later in the month she wore a stunning £795 Alice Temperley dress, again teamed with LK Bennett nude court shoes, when she and William watched Andy Murray win a match at Wimbledon. After meeting the royal couple, Murray told journalists: "If I'd known they were coming, I would have shaved. I was thinking to myself as I came off I was sweaty and very hairy. I said to them, 'I'm sorry, I'm a bit sweaty.' But it was very nice to get to meet them."

That summer, Catherine attended three weddings. Just hours after watching the Trooping the Colour, she zoomed down the M4 to join sister Pippa at the marriage of jockey Sam Waley-Cohen to party organizer Annabel Ballin in Lambourn, Berkshire. Sam was widely credited with saving William and Catherine's romance: stories circulated that he helped the couple rekindle their relationship following the split in 2007 – a claim he has modestly denied. Catherine was careful not to upstage the bride: her hat was the one she'd worn at that morning's ceremony and her dress was the spot-pattern black-and-white one

ABOVE: *The knights return to the State Apartments in open-top landaus. Here William and Catherine share a carriage with Prince Charles and the Duchess of Cornwall as they leave the Garter Service.*

she'd been photographed in at Boujis nightclub in London in 2007. She drove herself to the wedding, and she and Pippa chatted to guests and onlookers, later joining in making an avenue outside the church for the newlyweds.

On 25 September William and Catherine went to the wedding of their friends Harriet Colthurst and Thomas Sutton at Wilton in Wiltshire. The prince arrived early to serve as an usher and Catherine arrived with a friend, Louise Aubrey-Fletcher. The Duchess wore a mid-length raspberry-coloured lace dress by Collette Dinnigan with a matching pillbox hat and Prada pumps. The dress had first been worn by Carole Middleton at the Royal Academy's Summer Exhibition in 2009.

There was more royal clothes-recycling for the wedding of William's cousin Zara Phillips to England rugby player Mike Tindall in Edinburgh on 31 July. The evening before the wedding, Catherine joined other royal guests and friends for a reception on the Royal Yacht *Britannia*, wearing the green Diane Von Furstenberg dress first seen in Los Angeles earlier in the month. For the wedding she opted for a pale-gold dress she had worn for the 2006 nuptials of Camilla's daughter, Laura Parker Bowles, in Lacock, Wiltshire, with a dramatic tilted hat. On her feet were her by-now trademark nude pumps.

Another favourite outfit made a second appearance at the Thanksgiving

BELOW: *Queen Elizabeth II and Prince Philip pose with the Dean of Windsor, Reverend David Conner, after a church service at St George's Chapel, Windsor to mark Prince Philip's ninetieth birthday.*

Service at St George's Chapel, Windsor Castle to mark Prince Philip's ninetieth birthday: a pale-blue jacquard coat dress bought for the 2009 wedding of William's friend Nicholas van Cutsem to Alice Hadden-Paton. More mother–daughter sharing emerged as the jaunty blue Jane Corbett fascinator had been worn by Carole Middleton at Royal Ascot in June 2010.

Earlier in 2011 it had been reported that the Duchess told a friend she didn't want to be a "clothes horse" and intended to wear her outfits again and again. She was quoted as saying: "Times are tough; I cannot be expected to wear a new outfit for every royal engagement. I am not a fashion model."

Aspiring to normality in other respects too, Catherine likes to drive herself around London. Like Diana and other royal wives, she was given training by the SAS in emergency driving techniques in case of an ambush or terrorist incident.

For stays in London, William and Catherine were based at Nottingham Cottage, a small house in the grounds of Kensington Palace that was once home to the Queen's governess, Marion Crawford. Later it was announced that they would take over Apartment 1a, Kensington Palace, former home of Princess Margaret, near the apartment where William was brought up. The lavish four-storey home is protected by a walled garden and offers much-needed privacy.

ABOVE: *With former tennis champion Billie Jean King (in black) in the row behind, Catherine and William attend the fourth-round match between Andy Murray of Great Britain and Richard Gasquet of France on day seven of the Wimbledon Lawn Tennis Championships at the All England Lawn Tennis and Croquet Club on 27 June 2011.*

RIGHT: *The Duchess of Cambridge arrives for the wedding of Zara Phillips and Mike Tindall at Canongate Kirk in Edinburgh, 30 July 2011.*

CHARITABLE ENTERPRISES

Following their tour of North America, it was announced that William and Catherine would be scaling down their royal engagements partly because, according to a spokesperson for the Palace, "they are very conscious to make sure that the run-up to 2012 is the Queen's year", but also so William could resume his career and Catherine could spend time investigating the charities she wished to be associated with.

LEFT: *Catherine meets members of staff during a walkabout after opening the new Oak Centre for Children and Young People at Royal Marsden Hospital on 29 September 2011 in Sutton, Surrey.*

Nevertheless the couple made several appearances to support causes that were close to both their hearts, from visiting the Royal Marsden Hospital to supporting an appeal for the National Memorial Arboretum. Also during this time Catherine carried out her first solo engagement.

One of the key roles of the royal family is to reflect the nation's compassion during times of crisis, be those natural disasters or human atrocities. In 1996 the Queen memorably shed a tear when she laid flowers outside the school at Dunblane in Scotland where 16 children and a teacher were killed, while in 2011 William represented his grandmother when he flew to New Zealand to meet grieving families and thank emergency services following the devastating earthquake that killed 181 people in Christchurch.

BELOW: *The Queen and Princess Anne arrive on 17 March 1996 with a member of the Scottish Office to lay a wreath at the entrance of Dunblane Primary School, where a gunman had shot 16 children and a teacher four days earlier.*

RIGHT: *William and Catherine walking with the Lord Mayor of Birmingham, Councillor Anita Ward, on a visit to riot-affected areas at Summerfield Community Centre, Birmingham, on 19 August 2011.*

ABOVE: *Meeting Ajay and Monika Bhatia on 19 August 2011 at the Machan Express coffee bar in the centre of Birmingham, which had been ransacked during that summer's riots in the area. The Duke and Duchess of Cambridge also met the parents of the men of South Asian descent who were killed in the riots when they were mown down by a car in the ethnically mixed Winson Green area of the city.*

On 19 August 2011 William and Catherine met those affected by the summer riots in the Winson Green area of Birmingham. They met the parents of three men who were killed when they were mown down by a car as they tried to protect shops and homes from looters. Meanwhile Prince Harry met fire fighters in Manchester and Prince Charles toured areas affected by the riots in London, including Tottenham where the violence began.

After their 20-minute private meeting at Summerfield Community Centre, William and Catherine met local people affected by the riots as well as those who had helped victims afterwards. Mandy Sankey, nurse manager at Birmingham Children's Hospital, said the royal couple wanted to thank everyone for their hard work. She told reporters: "William said, 'We're sure you have already heard how grateful we are but we wanted to come here to say thank you in person.'"

Afterwards the Duke and Duchess drove to the city centre to visit the Machan Express coffee shop, which had lost £15,000 worth of stock during the riots but was still open for business the next day. William told the owner, Ajay Bhatia, "I am sorry this has happened to you."

Earlier, Derrick Campbell, a government adviser on anti-social behaviour and a community leader in Sandwell, said of the royal visit: "I think what came over really well was the human side to the royal family. It wasn't tokenistic, you could sense the genuine emotion that they showed and I think that really went a long way to reassuring us that these people really do care about what took place here."

At the end of September Catherine followed in Diana's footsteps by visiting the Royal Marsden Hospital in Surrey, where she and William, who is the hospital's president, opened the £18 million Oak Centre for Children and Young People. The Royal Marsden was especially important to the late Princess of Wales and it was here that she carried out her first solo engagement in 1982. She was also its president from 1989 until her death in 1997.

William and Catherine met young cancer sufferers and the prince took off his jacket and rolled up his sleeves to create the informal tone that characterized their visit. He posed for a photo with seven-year-old Ellis Andrews, who was

BELOW: *Charles and Camilla pose with volunteers from the Youth United network at the Croydon Voluntary Action Centre on 17 August 2011. They met residents and families whose homes and businesses were affected by the outbreaks of rioting and looting in the Croydon area.*

waiting for a bone-marrow transplant, while the Duchess chatted to Fabian Bate, aged nine, who was in the middle of four hours of chemotherapy.

A few weeks after the visit it emerged that Catherine had written a letter to Fabian, with whom she'd chatted for some time during her visit. The typed letter, which was signed "Catherine", said how much she had enjoyed meeting him and that she was "touched by his strength of character" and delighted to hear that one of his sisters was able to donate bone marrow to help him. She added, "I will keep my fingers crossed that your health goes from strength to strength in the coming months" and promised to keep him "in my thoughts and prayers".

LEFT: *Princess Diana (1961–97) wearing a Paul Costelloe suit and a hard hat at a topping-out ceremony at the Royal Marsden Hospital, London, June 1990.*

RIGHT, ABOVE: *William and Catherine meeting patient Digby Davidson, 14, as they open a children's cancer unit at the Royal Marsden Hospital in Sutton, Surrey, on 29 September 2011.*

RIGHT, BELOW: *The Duke and Duchess of Cambridge officially open the new Oak Centre for Children and Young People at the Royal Marsden Hospital on 29 September 2011.*

FOLLOWING PAGES, LEFT: *William poses with seven-year-old patient Ellis Andrews in the children's cancer unit of the Royal Marsden Hospital.*

FOLLOWING PAGES, RIGHT: *Catherine, Duchess of Cambridge speaks to guests at an event in support of the "In Kind Direct" charity at Clarence House, London on 26 October 2011. The event was her first solo engagement.*

Before the Royal Marsden visit, William, who had been up all night on a search and rescue mission, was quoted in the press as joking: "It was a bit of an early morning," before adding, "It's great to be here finally – we've been talking about this for a while." For the visit Catherine wore a sculpted £450 Amanda Wakeley oatmeal felt dress with three-quarter-length sleeves and her favourite LK Bennett nude high heels and matching clutch bag.

By now Catherine must have been aware that for those marrying into the royal family, charity dinners are a regular occurrence. The Duchess attended several during the autumn. In October she looked stunning in a red Beulah London evening gown at a fundraiser held at St James's Palace, organized by 100 Women in Hedge Funds. The event raised more than £675,000 for the Child Bereavement Charity, also an organization with which William is associated.

On 10 November, the royal couple attended another dinner at St James's Palace, this time in aid of the National Memorial Arboretum Future Foundations Appeal, of which William is a patron. Catherine looked stunning once again, wearing a silver Grecian-style gown designed by Jenny Packham, which was draped over one shoulder and gathered in at the waist. The addition of a bright red poppy, the emblem of Remembrance Day, added a dash of colour.

The dinner that made the most headlines was on 20 October when Catherine carried out her first solo engagement. She stood in for her father-in-law, Prince Charles, at short notice after the prince was suddenly required to fly to Saudi Arabia to present the Queen's condolences following the death of the Saudi Crown Prince.

The black-tie event was held at Clarence House for the charity In Kind Direct, which Charles founded in 1996 and which redistributes surplus goods from manufacturers and retailers to UK charities working both domestically and abroad. Catherine, dressed in an Amanda Wakeley gown, looked relaxed as she chatted to the 30 guests in the Garden Room before taking them through to dinner.

For once it wasn't Catherine's fashion that made headlines the next day but the fact that her swept-back hair revealed a seven-centimetre (three-inch) scar on her left temple, the result of a childhood operation. By chance, William has one in the same place, which he calls his Harry Potter scar, that was caused when a school friend accidentally hit him with a golf club.

In a statement released following the dinner, Catherine's spokesperson said: "She was so pleased that her first solo engagement was for the Prince of Wales, who has shown her so much support over the years." Robin Boles, the charity's chief executive, said Catherine was "completely natural, professional and charmed everyone. She spoke to every single guest and was genuinely interested in continuing to help."

ABOVE & RIGHT: *Attending a dinner reception in aid of the National Memorial Arboretum Appeal at St James's Palace in London, on 10 November 2011. The Appeal was launched in April 2009 by its patron, the Duke of Cambridge, to develop the Arboretum into a world-renowned centre for remembrance and to improve facilities for the 300,000 visiting families, servicemen and women, veterans and members of the public each year.*

TEAMWORK

———

The spring of 2012 would see Catherine taking on more solo royal appearances while William was deployed to the South Atlantic for six weeks. The Duchess also joined the Queen on two of her engagements in March, seeing for herself at first hand how the most experienced member of the royal family carries out her duties.

———

LEFT: *The Duchess waves as she arrives for an official visit to the Art Room facilities at Rose Hill Primary School in Oxford, on 21 February 2012. During her visit Catherine let slip to schoolchildren that her new puppy is called Lupo.*

After seeing in the New Year at Bucklebury with the Middletons, William and Catherine kept a low profile in January, only appearing officially in public once, when they attended the premiere of the film *War Horse*. Based on the children's novel by Michael Morpurgo, *War Horse* has enjoyed stage success in London's West End production, which both William and his grandparents, the Queen and Prince Philip, have been to see.

The premiere took place at the Odeon Leicester Square on 8 January, the eve of Catherine's thirtieth birthday. Looking stunning in an Alice Temperley cream dress with an outer layer of black lace patterned with leaves and flowers, the Duchess was shielded from the rain by an umbrella held aloft by Prince William.

The film's director, Steven Spielberg, was thrilled that William and Catherine could attend. "It's a very prestigious honour", he told the media beforehand, "because they represent an entirely new era in British royalty that has the entire world excited." The following day in an interview on *BBC Breakfast*, Spielberg revealed that Catherine had at one point discreetly shed a tear. "I was sitting next to her and all I know is at one point my wife, who was sitting to my right, right in front of my face she passed a Kleenex... I saw the Kleenex go across my face, arrive and stop but I didn't want to intrude on her experience watching *War Horse* so I never glanced over," he said. "According to my peripheral vision her eyes were dabbed."

There were no tears later in the month when the couple headed for the Caribbean island of Mustique for a family break with Catherine's parents, sister Pippa and brother James. They stayed in a property called Aurora House, which lies on the east coast of the island, costs £11,500 a week to hire and offers peace, seclusion and spectacular ocean views. Mustique was made famous by the late Princess Margaret, who built a villa, Les Jolies Eaux, on a secluded part of the island given to her as a wedding present by her friend Lord Glenconner. William and Catherine have also fallen in love with it and have holidayed there at least four times in the past.

In the first week of February, William arrived in the Falkland Islands for a six-week tour of duty as an RAF search and rescue pilot. The deployment, in the run-up to the thirtieth anniversary of the Falklands War of 1982, led to criticism by some Argentineans reported in the press that it constituted an "act of provocation" and that the prince would be wearing the uniform of a "conqueror" during his time there.

Meanwhile in the UK it was announced that Catherine would be undertaking some solo engagements during William's absence. In a statement released on 4 January, Catherine's office revealed that the Duchess would become patron of four organizations: Action on Addiction, East Anglia's Children's Hospices, The Art Room and the National Portrait Gallery, London. In addition she would become a volunteer in the Scout Association,

LEFT: *The Duke and Duchess attend the UK premiere of the film* War Horse *at the Odeon Leicester Square in London, on 8 January 2012.*

ABOVE: *Prince William and his crew prepare for their first sortie of a six-week deployment in the Mount Pleasant Complex on the Falkland Islands.*

LEFT: *The prince operates a Sea King Mk 3 helicopter during the search and rescue team's first sortie in the Falklands, on 4 February 2012. This was his first overseas operational deployment.*

RIGHT: *Catherine arrives at London's National Portrait Gallery to view the "Lucian Freud Portraits" exhibition on 8 February 2012.*

"volunteering time privately with groups in north Wales and elsewhere as opportunity arises". The statement concluded: "The Duchess has chosen to support organizations that complement the charitable work already undertaken by her husband."

Her first solo engagement occurred just a few days after William's departure. Catherine faced a blitz of camera flashes as she arrived at the National Portrait Gallery on the evening of 8 February to attend a preview of the "Lucian Freud Portraits" exhibition.

The following Tuesday, 14 February, she travelled to Liverpool in support of Alder Hey Children's Hospital and The Brink, an alcohol-free bar in the city centre that is run by the charity Action on Addiction. There she tried the latest drink on the menu, named the "Duchess" smoothie in her honour. "It's delicious," she told the crowds after tasting the £2.50 drink made from banana, almonds, milk, honey and cream.

It was, of course, Valentine's Day and she revealed that William had sent her a card from 12,700 kilometres (7,900 miles) away in the South Atlantic and had arranged for a bouquet of flowers to be delivered.

At Alder Hey some of the patients had made their own cards to give her. Ten-year-old Ethan Harris included a poem in his which read: "You're smiley like the sun, you're bright like a star, you're light when it's dark and I love your spark." A delighted Catherine said: "Thank you, that's lovely."

LEFT: *With William away in the South Atlantic, Catherine went on several day trips, including this one to Liverpool, where she visited the Alder Hey Children's Hospital on 14 February.*

ABOVE: *Catherine tries a specially made smoothie drink called "Duchess" during a visit to The Brink, an alcohol-free bar in Liverpool. The bar is run by one of the her charities, Action on Addiction.*

Exactly a week later, the Duchess spent the day at two Oxford schools, where – as patron of The Art Room – she joined schoolchildren who are experiencing emotional and behavioural problems. The charity uses art to increase their self-esteem and confidence. At Rose Hill Primary School, Catherine put on a denim apron with "Miss Catherine" stencilled across it as she helped five pupils paint scenes from Edward Lear's poem "The Owl and the Pussycat". Later Lisa Hancock, who manages the group, said Catherine "seemed to have as much fun as the children and seemed very relaxed and in her element, I think. She had all the right language and was very calm and gentle."

BELOW: *With William away, Catherine kept herself occupied on Valentine's Day. Here she unveils a plaque with patient Ethan Harris during her visit to Alder Hey Children's Hospital in Liverpool, 14 February 2012.*

The Duchess also visited the Oxford Spires Academy, for a discussion on the value of the sessions from past and present pupils. Julie Beattie, who founded The Art Room, said: "We are overwhelmed to have our Royal Patron here. We are a small charity, and to have that recognition is fantastic."

After her solo engagements, Catherine carried out two engagements with the Queen, at the latter's suggestion. A few weeks earlier, a senior aide had revealed: "The Duchess is keen to learn from the Queen and readily accepted the invitation to join her."

On 1 March, three generations of royal ladies – the Queen, Camilla Duchess of Cornwall and Catherine Duchess of Cambridge – travelled in the same car to visit Fortnum & Mason's store to mark the refurbishment of Piccadilly in central London. Inside, they toured different areas of the classic shop: the Queen viewed honey and preserves, Camilla toured the bakery section and Catherine was escorted to the tea area and the confectionary display. Later the royal party met for tea with 150 people involved in the Piccadilly regeneration. A week later, Catherine joined the Queen and Prince

ABOVE: *Catherine chats to Doctor Lisa Howell during her tour of the wards on her visit to Alder Hey Children's Hospital.*

Philip on the first day of their nationwide Diamond Jubilee tour in celebration of the Queen's 60 years on the throne. They travelled overnight on the royal train to Leicester, where the two royal ladies attended a student fashion show at De Montfort University, a multi-faith service at the cathedral and a short ceremony at the Clock Tower in the city centre, where the Queen received a gift to mark her Jubilee.

For Catherine it was part of a remarkable year, during which she had been transformed from being the shy bride accompanying Prince William on his engagements to taking on her own solo duties with ease and fitting seamlessly into royal life.

LEFT: *Catherine wears a personalized "Miss Catherine" apron during her visit to The Art Room facilities at Rose Hill Primary School, Oxford on 21 February 2012. As patron of The Art Room, a charity which works with children to increase their self-confidence and self-esteem, the Duchess visited two schools in Oxford.*

ABOVE: *Very much hands-on, Catherine spent two hours painting with children at Rose Hill Primary School, Oxford in her role as patron of The Art Room, proving she wants to be more than a mere figurehead.*

RIGHT: *A taste of things to come. Catherine views a Diamond-Jubilee-themed iced cake while visiting Fortnum & Mason store in Piccadilly on 1 March 2012.*

LEFT: *Three ladies in blue. Catherine, Camilla and the Queen outside the famous store Fortnum & Mason as Her Majesty prepares to unveil a plaque to mark the regeneration of London's Piccadilly on 1 March 2012.*

ABOVE: *Catherine joined the Queen and Prince Philip in Leicester on 8 March 2012 for the first leg of the Diamond Jubilee tour of Britain. The Queen is close to her granddaughter-in-law and regards her as a terrific asset to the monarchy.*

RIGHT: *The Queen and Catherine watch a fashion show together at De Montfort University; this was their first joint engagement of the day in Leicester on 8 March 2012.*

THE JUBILEE YEAR

The mood of patriotism and rejoicing generated by the royal wedding in 2011 continued the following year, when the Queen became only the second monarch in British history to celebrate a Diamond Jubilee and London hosted the 30th Olympic Games. The Golden Jubilee of 2002 had focused very much on the Queen: at the age of 76, the monarch had undertaken long-haul journeys to Australia, New Zealand, Canada and Jamaica as well as an exhausting tour of all parts of the United Kingdom. For the Diamond Jubilee of 2012, the Queen would rely on her family to shoulder some of the burden.

LEFT: *A private moment as Catherine comments to William during the Opening Ceremony of the Paralympic Games. They are flanked by Prime Minister David Cameron and his wife Samantha, Princess Anne and London Mayor Boris Johnson. Along with Prince Harry, the Cambridges were ambassadors for Team GB and Paralympic GB and attended as many events as they could.*

In December 2011 it was announced that in the following months the Queen and Prince Philip would carry out a series of regional visits, "travelling as widely as possible across England, Scotland, Wales and Northern Ireland". The palace statement went on to reveal that the Queen had asked members of the royal family to represent her in Commonwealth countries, Crown Dependencies and British Overseas Territories. The Prince of Wales and the Duchess of Cornwall would head for Australia, Canada, New Zealand and Papua New Guinea. Prince Harry would represent his grandmother in Belize, Jamaica and the Bahamas, where his fun-loving side rapidly won hearts among Her Majesty's most chilled-out subjects. Prince William and Catherine were to fly the flag in Malaysia, Singapore, the Solomon Islands and Tuvalu. This wouldn't be until September 2012 and, in the meantime, the Cambridges were to support the Queen nearer home.

On 1 March 2012, Catherine and Camilla joined the Queen on a visit to a flagship London store, Fortnum & Mason, where they enjoyed a tour of the famous food halls. They were presented with hampers containing chocolate

PREVIOUS PAGES: *Caherine smiles through. Senior royals joined a flotilla of 1,000 boats in a Thames River Pageant on 3 June 2012 as part of the Queen's Diamond Jubilee celebrations. Heavy rain failed to mar the event as thousands lined the river.*

BELOW: *Flying the flag. William and Catherine get into the spirit of the occasion as they attend the Diamond Jubilee concert in front of Buckingham Palace.*

RIGHT: *The Royal Family leaving St Paul's Cathedral following the official Thanksgiving Service to mark the Queen's 60 years as monarch. Although the event was marred by the absence of the Duke of Edinburgh, the Queen's four children and seven grandchildren were there to offer support.*

truffles, handmade preserves and dog biscuits, appropriate gifts for three generations of dog-lovers.

A week later the Duchess joined the Queen and Prince Philip on the first day of their Jubilee tour of the UK, which began in Leicester. The royal party travelled by train from London and enjoyed, among other things, a fashion show at De Montfort University, where the Queen and Catherine sat side by side and exchanged comments throughout. The invitation to join the royal party was an opportunity for the Duchess to learn the ropes from the two most experienced members of the family. It was also perhaps a reflection on the Queen's part that Diana had not been given such support in the early days of her marriage.

The Cambridges joined the Queen on another visit to the Midlands when, on 13 June, the three of them carried out a walkabout in Nottingham's Old Market Square. Later they visited Vernon Park in Basford where the monarch unveiled a plaque conferring Queen Elizabeth II Fields in Trust status on the park.

Earlier in the month, the Cambridges had been present at three key events during the Diamond Jubilee weekend. On Saturday 2 June they boarded the *Spirit of Chartwell*, which acted as a lavishly decorated royal barge, taking the royal party from Chelsea to the Tower of London in an unforgettable, if rainy, river pageant. While other members of the royal family joined the flotilla, the *Spirit of Chartwell*'s VIP guest list was limited to the Queen and Prince Philip, Prince Charles and Camilla, the Cambridges and Prince Harry.

Sadly Prince Philip succumbed to a bladder infection and was unable to attend the Jubilee Concert held in front of Buckingham Palace on Monday evening, which was watched by three generations of royals, including the Cambridges.

The royal line of succession was the focus following the Thanksgiving Service at

St Paul's Cathedral on 5 June. The Queen, Charles, Camilla, William, Kate and Harry went on to a lunch hosted by livery companies in Westminster Hall. They returned to Buckingham Palace in a carriage procession before appearing on the balcony to watch an RAF flypast and a celebratory cascade of gunfire, known as a *feu de joie*, from soldiers massed in the palace forecourt. The fact that the Queen chose only those in the direct line of succession to appear on the balcony with her was seen as emphasizing the future during celebrations that had necessarily focused on the past.

William, Catherine and Harry were also destined to play a significant role in the other major spectacle of 2012 – the Olympic Games. The previous November it had been announced that the three young royals would become ambassadors for Team GB and Paralympic GB. Prince William said the three of them were honoured to be asked to help and added, "We are hugely looking forward to this incredible sporting competition, but are also looking beyond next summer's Games to the springboard it will provide for future success and excellence."

BELOW: *A slimmed-down balcony scene. The Queen asked only her heir and his heir to join her on the palace balcony with their wives and Prince Harry after the Jubilee service. The message was clear: while we celebrate the past, this is the future.*

This would be Catherine's first national role, as she had yet to announce which charities she would support. It was an ideal royal duty for her as she had been proficient in many sports at school. This love of sport had helped her forge a strong bond with William during their years at the University of St Andrews.

Catherine proved to be an active ambassador, in July attending a reception at the National Portrait Gallery to launch "Road to 2012", an exhibition that showed top athletes and key figures involved in the planning of the Games.

On the evening before the Games opened, the royal trio of William, Catherine and Harry sported their official Team GB polo shirts to watch the Olympic Flame being handed over outside Buckingham Palace in the final stages prior to being carried to the Olympic Stadium.

The following afternoon the Cambridges were present at a Buckingham Palace reception hosted by the Queen to welcome visiting dignitaries. Wearing an ice-blue Christopher Kane outfit, Kate more than held her own in the room full of stylish women, including Princess Charlene of Monaco and US First Lady Michelle Obama, whom she had met at the palace during the American state visit in May 2011.

After the reception the guests and the UK royals headed for the opening of the Games at the Olympic Stadium in Stratford. "The Queen" memorably arrived by

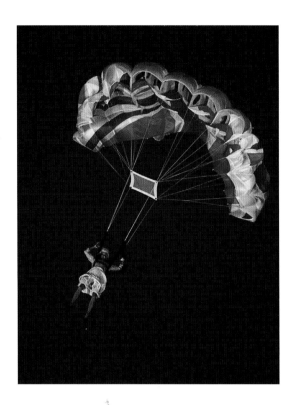

helicopter, much to the surprise of her grandsons who had been kept in the dark about her James Bond act. In his autobiography, *Running My Life*, Sebastian Coe recalled that the princes were "beside themselves" as the stunt double jumped from the helicopter dressed as the monarch, adding that "as she started her descent two voices shouted out in unison behind me 'Go Granny!'"

After the Opening Ceremony, Catherine came to support Team GB on nine occasions, sometimes with William or Harry and often alone. Probably the most memorable photos of Catherine at the Olympics were taken when she and William were at the Velodrome to watch Chris Hoy successfully compete for his fifth Olympic gold medal. When he crossed the finishing line, the Cambridges threw themselves into each other's arms in total delight.

Both the Queen and Prince Charles absented themselves from the Closing Ceremony, at which Harry and Catherine were to fly the royal flag. The Duchess wore a printed silk Whistles dress as she chatted to Prime Minister David Cameron and Lord Coe before taking her seat.

Catherine was also present when the Queen opened the Paralympic Games on 29 August and attended several events over the following days.

On 11 September William and Catherine arrived in Singapore to represent the Queen during her Diamond Jubilee year. The first stage of the tour was overshadowed by an international row that blew up when photos taken of a topless Duchess relaxing at Viscount Linley's chateau in France were published

LEFT, TOP: *Stuntman Gary Connery dressed as the Queen pulls the rip cord on a Union Jack parachute – an unforgettable way to herald the monarch's arrival at the Olympic Stadium.*

LEFT, BOTTOM: *William and Catherine applaud as the Queen opens the 2012 Olympic Games in London on 27 July. Politicians past and present joined the VIPs including David Cameron and his wife Samantha.*

ABOVE: *Royal Support. Sophie Countess of Wessex, Princess Anne's husband Sir Tim Laurence, Catherine and William watch cycling events in the Velodrome on Day 6 of the Games.*

in the French edition of *Closer* magazine in what the royal couple said was "a grotesque and totally unjustifiable invasion of privacy". While William looked preoccupied and irritated at times during the early stages of the tour, Catherine smiled serenely and didn't seem as concerned.

The tour moved on to Malaysia, the Solomon Islands and Tuvalu, the last giving the press its most memorable images of the Diamond Jubilee tour. On Tuvalu the couple were carried from their aircraft on a "carriage" made of leaves on the shoulders of 25 strapping locals. Later Catherine covered her Alice Temperley dress in a grass skirt and donned a flower crown as the royal couple sashayed to a traditional Polynesian welcome.

They arrived back in London on 20 September where, after a year of appearing centre stage in Jubilee and Olympic ceremonial events, the couple could turn their thoughts to the more personal matter of starting a family.

LEFT: *An ecstatic royal couple hug each other after legendary cyclist Sir Chris Hoy wins a gold medal in the Men's Team Sprint at the Velodrome on 2 August.*

BELOW: *Catherine proved herself a worthy ambassador for Britain when she and Prince William represented the Queen on a tour of Southeast Asia. Here the Duchess delivers a speech at Hospis Malaysia on the third day of the visit.*

PREGNANCY ANNOUNCEMENTS

William and Catherine made no secret of their desire to have a baby. The topic was raised during their engagement interview in November 2010 when Catherine agreed that family was very important to her, adding: "I hope we will be able to have family ourselves." Interviewer Tom Bradby asked them if they wanted lots of children and William replied for both of them: "I think we'll take it one step at a time. We'll sort of get over the marriage first and then maybe look at the kids."

LEFT: *The smiles of relief that say all's well. William and Kate leave the King Edward VII Hospital, London, where the Duchess had been treated for acute morning sickness, 6 December 2012.*

Historically the first royal baby has tended to arrive around a year or so after the wedding. Prince Charles was born on 14 November 1948, six days before his parents' first wedding anniversary. William himself was born on 21 June 1982, over a month before Charles and Diana's first anniversary on 29 July.

Given the fact that, as we have seen, the couple played a central part in the Diamond Jubilee and Olympic events, 2012 was unlikely to see a royal birth. This didn't deter the press pack that follow William and Catherine's every move from scrutinizing them for telltale signs.

In early November 2011, just over six months after the royal wedding, the Duchess fuelled rumours that she was pregnant by politely declining to taste some peanut paste during a visit to Denmark. Expectant mothers are advised not to eat peanuts in case it triggers an allergy in their children. An aide confirmed: "There was no reason for her not tasting it, she does not have an allergy," but this didn't stop rumours going into overdrive when Catherine was

LEFT: *Prince William was a constant visitor to his wife's well-guarded bedside. Worldwide delight at the news of Catherine's pregnancy was tempered by the fact that she was forced to go into hospital so early on.*

observed patting or holding her stomach at least a dozen times during the royal trip to an aid centre in Copenhagen.

In the course of the official visit to Singapore in September 2012, Catherine again sent the press pack into a frenzy of speculation by twice toasting the health of the Queen using mineral water, rather than the usual wine, at a state banquet. The newspapers duly reported that pregnant mothers are advised to avoid alcohol.

On 28 November the royal couple visited Cambridge on what turned out to be another baby-themed day. During a walkabout Catherine met Tessa Davies and her baby son, James William, and said, "Hello, cute little man," to the seven-month-old, who was named after the prince, before tickling his feet.

Meanwhile, further down the same street, William was handed a baby-gro by mum Samantha Morton. The baby-gro bore a picture of a helicopter and the legend "Daddy's little co-pilot", which thrilled the Search and Rescue-trained prince. "I'll keep that!" said a delighted William and handed it to an aide.

At this stage, only William and Catherine would have realized the rumours were true and that she indeed was pregnant. However, the news would break in a way that neither would have wanted. During the afternoon of Monday, 3 December 2011, William and Catherine's office at St James's Palace released the following statement:

"Their Royal Highnesses the Duke and Duchess of Cambridge are very pleased to announce that the Duchess of Cambridge is expecting a baby. The Queen, the Duke of Edinburgh, the Prince of Wales, the Duchess of Cornwall and Prince Harry and members of both families are delighted with the news."

However, the statement went on to say that the Duchess was suffering from hyperemesis gravidarum, which requires supplementary hydration and nutrients, and that she had therefore been taken to the King Edward VII Hospital in London. The statement added: "As the pregnancy is in its very early stages, Her Royal Highness is expected to stay in hospital for several days and will require a period of rest thereafter."

The palace wouldn't say how many weeks pregnant the Duchess was, although it confirmed that she hadn't yet reached the crucial 12-week stage. Neither would it say when the couple had discovered the news, other than "recently". Catherine had been staying with her parents at the weekend when she developed acute morning sickness, one of the key symptoms of hyperemesis gravidarum, which can lead to dehydration.

On the previous Friday she had visited her old prep school, St Andrew's School, Pangbourne, where she took part in an energetic game of hockey despite wearing high-heeled boots, which suggested nothing was amiss at that stage and that her illness had come on over the weekend.

The couple had intended to keep news of the pregnancy a family secret until Catherine had reached 12 weeks. After she was hospitalized, however, they decided it would be better to make an announcement in order to avoid any speculation about her condition.

As so easily happens these days, the news became global within hours. Prime minister David Cameron tweeted: "I'm delighted by the news that the Duke & Duchess of Cambridge are expecting a baby. They will make wonderful parents." Even the White House paid tribute, President Barack Obama's press secretary Jay Carney saying, "On behalf of everyone here... beginning with the President and First Lady, we extend our congratulations to the Duke and Duchess of Cambridge on the welcome news we received from London that they are expecting their first child."

William's uncle Earl Spencer said: "It is wonderful news and I am thrilled for them both." This comment from the Spencer family was a reminder that the baby would, of course, have been Princess Diana's first grandchild.

During her stay in hospital the Duchess was visited daily by Prince William and also by her parents, brother James and sister Pippa. On the second day of her stay hospital staff were the victims of a practical joke by an Australian radio station. DJs Mel Greig and Michael Christian called the King Edward VII Hospital pretending to be the Queen and Prince Charles, and were surprised when their call was transferred to the private nurse looking after the Duchess, who gave them general details of the patient's health.

After the taped call was broadcast it rapidly caused a media storm. A spokesman for the hospital condemned the stunt as "a foolish prank call that we all deplore". He added, "We take patient confidentiality extremely seriously and we are now reviewing our telephone protocols."

ABOVE: *During Catherine's stay, nurses at King Edward VII Hospital were duped by presenters from Australia's 2day FM radio station who pretended to be the Queen and Prince Charles. The stunt would have tragic consequences.*

RIGHT: *Looking tired but managing a smile, Catherine emerged from the main entrance of the hospital and told waiting journalists, "I'm feeling much better." She was driven to her home at Nottingham Cottage, in the grounds of Kensington Palace, to recuperate.*

LEFT: *Bookmakers wasted no time in taking bets on the name of the new royal baby. Here one enterprising bookie offers odds outside the King Edward Hospital, with Victoria and George as the current favourites.*

The only member of the family to speak publicly about the call was the Prince of Wales, who made light of it. Asked by reporters how he felt about Catherine's pregnancy, Charles raised his eyebrows and joked: "How do you know I'm not a radio station?" Prince Charles then revealed his delight about the news of the pregnancy: "I'm thrilled, marvellous," adding: "A very nice thought of grandfatherhood at my old age, if I may say so. So that's splendid. And I'm very glad my daughter-in-law is getting better, thank goodness."

Sadly the prank had tragic consequences when it emerged that 46-year-old Jacintha Saldanha, the nurse who took the call from the DJs and transferred it to Catherine's floor, had committed suicide. It later emerged that she had hanged herself and left suicide notes, one of which condemned the stunt.

The Duke and Duchess of Cambridge said in a statement they were "deeply saddened" by the death of the nurse. St James's Palace said that the royal couple "were looked after so wonderfully well at all times by everybody at King Edward VII Hospital, and their thoughts and prayers are with Jacintha Saldanha's family, friends and colleagues at this very sad time." A palace spokesman later added further confirmation that "at no point did the palace complain to the hospital about the incident. On the contrary, we offered our full and heartfelt support to the nurses involved and hospital staff at all times."

The duchess had left the hospital the day before the nurse's death. She was discharged at 10.45am on Thursday, 6 December and looked pale as she posed for photographs on the steps of the hospital. Dressed in a blue Diane von Furstenberg coat and holding a dazzling bunch of yellow flowers, she managed a warm smile to the assembled media and said: "I'm feeling much better." The couple then left in a black Jaguar for their London home, in the grounds of Kensington Palace, to rest and recuperate and to look forward to the birth of their much-wanted baby.

BELOW: *Having resumed her duties, a pregnant Catherine appears smitten by this baby girl while on a walkabout in Glasgow on 4 April 2013, although the cute centre of attention seems more keen on the contents of the bouquet than the royal visitor.*

Clarence House released news of Kate's second pregnancy on Monday, 8 September 2014, and once again it came with a certain amount of drama. For a second time, the Duke and Duchess were forced to announce the news before Kate had passed the significant 12-week milestone. The reason the news broke at breakfast time that day was because Kate had been due to accompany William on a visit to Oxford to formally open a £21 million China study centre at Oxford University, but she was suffering from acute morning sickness and would not be able to attend.

The news read: "Their Royal Highnesses The Duke and Duchess of Cambridge are very pleased to announce that The Duchess of Cambridge is expecting their second child."

"The Queen and members of both families are delighted with the news."

"As with her first pregnancy, The Duchess is suffering from Hyperemesis Gravidarum. Her Royal Highness will no longer accompany The Duke of Cambridge on their planned engagement in Oxford today. The Duchess of Cambridge is being treated by doctors at Kensington Palace."

Her doctors are the surgeon gynaecologist to the Queen, Alan Farthing, and the surgeon gynaecologist to the royal household, Guy Thorpe-Beeston. Hyperemesis gravidarum affects about 15 per cent of all pregnancies. It causes severe vomiting – sometimes up to 30 times a day – and can lead to dehydration and weight loss, and Kate, once again, needed intravenous feeding and fluids.

Official news of the pregnancy came just 48 hours after the couple told the Queen and senior royals as well as the Middleton family. Certainly there seemed no sign that Kate was suffering any illness when she was snapped arriving by train at London's King Cross Station on 29 August. She and William had spent a fortnight in Norfolk overseeing the improvements on Anmer Hall, two miles from Sandringham House, which had been given to them as a country retreat by the Queen. While the prince led the way with their dog Lupo, Kate followed behind carrying two heavy shoulder bags.

William carried out the visit to Oxford, arriving at 1.30pm, just a few hours after news of the pregnancy was released. By then Twitter was in overdrive and the Prime Minister, David Cameron, was one of the first VIPs to tweet good wishes: "Many congratulations to the Duke and Duchess of Cambridge. I'm delighted by the happy news that they're expecting another baby."

The Archbishop of Canterbury, Justin Welby, who is used to leading prayers for the health of the royal family tweeted: "Wonderful news that the Duke & Duchess of Cambridge are expecting second child. Praying for the family, and that morning sickness subsides."

William looked happy and relaxed in Oxford, and didn't cut back on his two- hour visit, to rush back to Kensington Palace, though he admitted that "it had been a tricky few days." Elsewhere Prince Harry was more upbeat, joking: "I can't wait to see my brother suffer more," and adding that the news

was "exciting. I hope the two of them have the opportunity to go through the process again with a little bit of peace and quiet." He also thought, "George will be over the moon. I think he will be thrilled having another small younger brother or sister."Asked if he minded dropping to fifth in line to the throne as a result of the birth, the prince laughed and replied: "Great!"

Kate's indisposition meant that she had to pull out of supporting Harry's hugely successful Invictus Games, a Paralympic style sports event for injured and sick service personnel. She also reluctantly pulled out of her first solo overseas tour, to represent the Queen at the 50th anniversary celebrations of Malta's independence, though the Duke stood in for her.

On 20 October Kensington Palace released a statement that told the world the baby was due in April, suggesting that Kate had reached the crucial 12-week stage at the time of the announcement. The palace revealed she was still suffering from morning sickness but that her condition was "steadily improving". As she got better she opted to stay with her parents at Bucklebury, where Carole Middleton was said to have researched alternative remedies including herbal tea.

ABOVE: *The smiling and radiant Duchess at her first public appearance on 21 October 2014, following the announcement of her second pregnancy. The couple are seen as they welcome the President of Singapore Tony Tan Keng Yam at the Royal Garden Hotel in London. Due to extreme morning sickness the Duchess had to miss a string of summer engagements.*

The Duchess made her first public appearance on 21 October when she and William officially welcomed Singapore's President Tony Tan as he and his wife began a four-day State Visit to the UK. Kate looked remarkably well as she met the couple at their hotel near to Kensington Palace. When Mrs Tan said she was glad Kate could make the engagement, the Duchess replied: "So am I. I've been looking forward to getting out of the house, that's for sure." The Cambridges accompanied the VIP guests to Horse Guards Parade for the formal introduction to the Queen and members of the government. They then drove the short distance to Buckingham Palace in the Scottish State Coach, built in 1830. William stayed on for the lunch party hosted by his grandmother, but Kate returned to Kensington Palace to rest before appearing later in the day at the Natural History Museum. The Duchess is the museum's patron and she joined other guests, including Sir David Attenborough at the Wildlife Photographer of the Year 2014 awards ceremony.

By November Kate was well enough to travel to Pembroke to visit a refinery with William before they headed for the Wales v Australia rugby match at Cardiff.

A sign that she was fighting fit in the middle stages of pregnancy, just as she was with George, became clear when Kate accompanied William on a 48-hour whirlwind visit to the USA on 7 December. The only concession to her pregnancy was that the Duchess was based in New York throughout, whereas William flew to Washington for a meeting with President Obama on the morning after their arrival.

Kate stayed remarkably slim as the weeks went by, though when congratulated on looking so beautiful by a well-wisher outside Sandringham Church on Christmas Day she joked that she "felt big".

ABOVE: *The Duchess gives well-wishers and fans a glimpse of her growing bump in her pale blue Matthew Williams coat on a visit to the oil refinery in Pembroke, Wales, in November 2014.*

LEFT: *Patron of The Natural History Museum, Catherine, Duchess of Cambridge leaves the museum after attending the Wildlife Photographer of The Year 2014 Awards ceremony in October 2014, in London. Wearing a stunning Jenny Packham dress she met the finalists, viewed the exhibition and joined Sir David Attenborough to present the awards.*

MATERNITY STYLE

Catherine's style has been a talking point for over a decade, since it was first rumoured she was dating Prince William. Interest in her fashions grew and grew following their wedding and, once it was announced the future queen was pregnant, it went into overdrive. Magazines, blogs, tabloids and tweets have analysed, praised and occasionally criticized her maternity wardrobe. Until the 1970s royal pregnancies were a no-go area for the media. The mother-to-be withdrew from public life four or five months before the arrival of the blue-blooded baby.

LEFT: *Catherine wore an apricot coloured Tara Jarmon Coat and a peach dress by a private dress maker during her visit to Naomi House Children's Hospice in Hampshire on 29 April 2013, her second wedding anniversary.*

LEFT: *The Duchess wore a teal Malene Birger coat with black trim, black Cornelia James gloves and matching Episode Angel suede shoes for her visit to Baker Street Underground Station with the Queen and Prince Philip on 20 March 2013.*

Only a few public photos exist of the Queen visibly pregnant, and in those she is shielded from the gaze of her subjects by fur coats or thick jackets. Fun-loving Princess Margaret gave up royal duties but continued to party until late in both her pregnancies. Photos were snapped of her leaving nightclubs and theatres, but deferential British newspaper editors refrained from using them.

It was Princess Anne who broke the taboo. She made no attempt to hide her baby bulge when she was expecting her son Peter. One newspaper carried a front-page photo of her at an equestrian meeting under the heading "She Doesn't Give a Damn!". Over three years later and pregnant again, Anne was photographed attending the wedding of her sister-in-law Sarah Phillips on 9 May 1981, just six days before giving birth to Zara.

As with Catherine, Princess Diana's pregnancies were of endless interest to the press and she joked, "The whole world is watching my stomach!" Both her sons were born in summer – William in June 1982 and Harry in September 1984 – so Diana resorted to comfortable smock dresses, many made by some of her favourite Chelsea-based designers, Bellville Sassoon and Catherine Walker.

Catherine's good abdominal muscles may explain why she was nearly six months pregnant before she began to show, and had no reason to consider maternity wear until then. After leaving hospital, her first public engagement

was on 16 December 2012, when she appeared at the Sports Personality of the Year Awards in London to present Bradley Wiggins with the Sports Personality trophy and a Life Achievement Award to Lord Sebastian Coe. Looking her usual svelte self and remarkably well after her hospital stay, she stunned the audience in a bottle-green Alexander McQueen gown designed by Sarah Burton, the creator of her wedding dress, who had just collected her OBE from Buckingham Palace. The floor-length crepe wool gown had a daring thigh-high slit at the front and a swooping V-neck, bell-sleeves and a *trompe l'oeil* belt waistband. A black version of the dress was on sale the same week for £1,000. Catherine had opted for Jimmy Choo heels and her jewellery included an Asprey button pendant and Kiki McDonough blue topaz earrings, to match her sapphire engagement ring.

On 11 January 2013 Catherine wore a high-waisted burgundy dress by Whistles for a private viewing at the National Portrait Gallery of her first official portrait, by artist Paul Emsley. She told the artist: "It's just amazing. I thought it was brilliant." Prince William, who accompanied her, added: "It's beautiful, it's absolutely beautiful."

Catherine's baby bump made its official debut on 19 February when the Duchess, as patron of Action on Addiction, visited Hope House near Clapham Common in London. Now in her fourth month of pregnancy, she wore a £298 MaxMara monochrome wrap dress, with a grey slip underneath. She teamed it with a pair of black platform court shoes and a 167-button pendant necklace by Asprey.

March saw the Duchess appear in both new and recycled outfits to combat chilly weather. On 5 March she wore a favourite design, a burgundy Hobbs Celeste coat, teamed with a pleated dress from Great Plains, for a day of engagements in Grimsby. Ten days later she attended Cheltenham Gold Cup wearing a peach-camel-coloured coat, which she had worn before her marriage,

ABOVE: *The Duchess recycled the red Armani coat she wore for Prince William's graduation ceremony from Sandhurst in December 2006, for a visit to Dumfries House in Ayrshire in March 2012. North of the border, the Cambridges are known as the Earl and Countess of Strathearn, and her scarf is made using the Strathearn tartan.*

and a brown Betty Boop hat from Lock & Co which she'd worn twice before. She also wore a pair of £488 Aquatalia by Marvin K brown boots.

There was more royal recycling on St Patrick's Day, 17 March, when Catherine presented shamrocks to the Irish Guards. She opted for the £1,150 emerald-green Emilia Wickstead dress-coat she had worn for the same ceremony a year earlier. This time she removed the shiny black belt and wore a black cashmere polo neck and thick opaque tights. Catherine continued to wear high heels throughout her pregnancy and on this occasion she caught her left heel in a grate and, laughing, had to hold on to Prince William as she pulled it out.

Another Catherine trait during pregnancy was short hemlines. Her bump may have been discreetly hidden but her well-toned legs were not. On a visit to Buckinghamshire on 19 March, the five-months-pregnant Duchess teamed a £45 Topshop black-collar dress with a dazzling £560 cream coat by Goa. She wore another short coat the following day on a visit with the Queen to Baker Street tube station to mark its 150th anniversary.

The Duchess wore Le Chameau wellies and her favourite blue skinny jeans when she took a trip to the Lake District to visit the Great Tower Scout Activity Centre. She also donned a khaki-green jacket and matching woollen hat, appropriate for her role as an occasional volunteer with the Scout Association.

At six months pregnant, Catherine reviewed the National Parade of Queen's Scouts at Windsor Castle in a £1,750 Mulberry frayed coat of mint-green tweed. Two days later, her burgeoning waistline was evident at a school in Wythenshawe, Greater Manchester, in a clingy £1,065 Erdem dress with a bold Visconti print.

ABOVE: *For the annual National Parade of Queen's Scouts, Catherine wore a Mulberry frayed coat in mint-green tweed, with a Whiteley Cappuccino hat she originally wore at the 2011 Derby and her favourite nude LK Bennett shoes.*

RIGHT: *The Duchess wore a sleeveless pale-blue Emilia Wickstead dress for a reception in aid of one of her charities, The Art Room, held at the National Portrait Gallery on 24 April. The silk-blend full-skirted summer dress with an empire waist was specially made for Catherine and she looked radiant as she smiles for the cameras.*

One of her most striking maternity outfits was a polka-dot Topshop dress, worn with a Ralph Lauren jacket to visit Warner Brothers Studio. The dress sold out in hours and Catherine wore it again a few weeks later for the Oxfordshire wedding of her friends William van Cutsem and Rosie Ruck Keene.

Out of respect to the Queen, Catherine usually wears something more formal when she accompanies her grandmother-in-law. On 22 May, at a Buckingham Palace garden party, she opted for a £1,285 canary-yellow coat by Emilia Wickstead. Two weeks later, for a Thanksgiving Service in Westminster Abbey to mark the 60th anniversary of the Queen's coronation, she chose a nude Jenny Packham dress with matching coat and a Jane Taylor pillbox hat.

For her last solo engagement – naming the cruise liner *Royal Princess* at Southampton – Catherine wore a dramatic £169 Dalmatian-print coat from Hobbs, with a black hat and matching LK Bennett heels. Once again "the Kate effect" was evident: the dress sold out in all sizes within minutes. Two days later, on her final official appearance before the birth, Catherine came back to Alexander McQueen, picking a pastel-pink coat with a matching hat by Jane Corbett.

BELOW: Catherine used both designer and high-street fashion throughout her pregnancy. One of the most talked about was this £38 polka-dot Topshop design, worn under a Ralph Lauren jacket for the royal visit to Warner Brothers Studio in Hertfordshire, including the set of the Harry Potter films, on 26 April.

RIGHT: The sun may have failed to shine but Catherine looks summery in this canary-yellow coat designed by Emilia Wickstead at a Buckingham Palace Garden Party on 22 May. She teamed it with a Jane Corbett hat and her favourite nude heels.

FOLLOWING PAGES: Elegant even in advanced pregnancy, Catherine joins the royal family on the balcony at Buckingham Palace to watch the flypast for the Trooping of the Colour in June.

LEFT: *Three days after the announcement of her second pregnancy, Kate attended the Action on Addiction Autumn Gala Evening. During the dinner she spoke to Swede Hans Rausing and met with many charity supporters. She was joined by comedian and impressionist Rory Bremner.*

LEFT: *For their final overseas engagement in 2014, the royal couple went to New York for three days on 8 December. On their second day, they attended the Cleveland Cavaliers vs. Brooklyn Nets game at Barclays Center in Brooklyn, where they met and were photographed with the basketball player LeBron James.*

Kate looked elegant and chic when she undertook her first royal engagement since her second pregnancy was announced. The Cambridges officially welcomed the President of Singapore and his wife at the start of their three-day State Visit to the UK. The Duchess wore a grey Alexander McQueen coat, with a fitted bodice, full skirt and a nipped-in waist, showing no sign of a baby bump at this stage.

Kate teamed it with a Jane Taylor grey velour felt beret that she had previously worn during their visit to Australia earlier this year. She carried a black suede Jenny Packham handbag that matched her black suede Prada shoes.

Later in the day she wore another stunning outfit that made her first day back in the limelight a totally stylish one. She arrived at the Natural History Museum in a pale blue wrap front maxi dress by Jenny Packham with a V-neck and a daring side split. She teamed it with beige high heels decorated with a bow on the side and a matching box clutch bag.

For her third engagement, later the same week, Kate wore a black Alice Temperley cocktail dress for a dinner and reception in aid of Action on Addiction at London's L'Anima Restaurant. The "emblem flare" dress has daring slashed nude panels at the front and back and retails at £595.

In early November she wore a light blue Matthew Williamson coat with heeled boots for a tour of a refinery in Pembroke and a visit to Cardiff's Millennium Stadium to watch the rugby.

Kate was around 16 weeks pregnant when she attended the Royal Variety Performance at the London Palladium, wearing a black lace Diane von Furstenberg gown. She teamed it with a classic black clutch bags and pearl earrings.

Black was the choice again at a Kensington Palace reception for the Place2Be charity. This time she wore a spotted black top from the High Street store Hobbs and a Jenny Packham skirt.

The Duchess pulled out all the stops for her short visit to New York in early December when she was nearly five months pregnant. For her arrival she wore a rich plum coat by the British maternity label Seraphine. She later changed into a black lace cocktail dress by Beulah London, which was founded in 2011 by William's friend Lady Natasha Rufus Isaacs.

On the day after their arrival, the couple attended an NBA game featuring the Brooklyn Nets and met Beyoncé and husband Jay-Z. Kate paid a fashion tribute to the host nation by wearing a grey bouclé coat from American designer Tory Burch together with skinny jeans and black heels.

LEFT: *On their New York tour, the Duke and Duchess visited one of the city's most somber sites, the National September 11 Memorial. The Duchess laid a wreath of white roses and paid personal tribute to those who lost their lives in the 2001 terrorist attacks.*

RIGHT: *For their final engagement in New York, the couple attended an evening at the Metropolitan Museum of Art – the St Andrews University 600th anniversary appeal dinner. The Duchess wore a midnight blue Jenny Packham evening gown and the cut of the dress meant that the Duchess's baby bump was more visible that at previous engagements.*

On their final day in the USA, the Duchess brightened up a rain-soaked New York by wearing a bright pink Mulberry coat that retails at £1,500, about $2,500.

Kate is never afraid to recycle her favourite outfits and for her final appearance of the tour – a fundraiser in aid of St Andrews University, where the royal couple met – she wore a midnight blue Jenny Packham dress. She has worn it twice before, but it looked stunning as she descended the steps of the Metropolitan Museum of Art. She also wore with it some fabulous diamond and emerald earrings and a matching bracelet.

Back in the UK, it was not haute couture but a hoodie for Kate's next engagement. She was in East London to visit the 23rd Poplar Beaver Scout Colony and wore a black UK Scouting hooded top with black skinny J Brand jeans and Stuart Weitzman knee high boots.

For her final public appearance of 2014 at church on Christmas Day, Kate wore a rustic tweed "Turpin Coat" from the British designer Moloh, which was on sale for £685 in the spring of 2013. It highlights another Kate fashion fad – to delay wearing something she has purchased one or more years ago.

LEFT: *In January 2015, the Duchess visited the new Kensington Leisure Centre. She wore a baby-blue cashmere coat from the label Seraphine. Kate was six months pregnant and revealed that the baby was pretty active. "It's moving all the time. I can feel it kicking now."*

LEFT: *For one of her final appearances before the birth of her second child, the Duchess visited the set of the long-running telelvsion drama* Downton Abbey. *Wearing a cream Jojo Maman Bebe coat, she was shown the servant's bells by actor Brendan Coyle who plays John Bates.*

Kate remained typically stylish throughout the later stages of her second pregnancy, and, as with the earlier months, she wore both High Street and designer wear.

For her first engagement of 2015 she wore a striking loose-fitting maternity dress by Madderson for her visit to Barlby Primary School in London where she officially opened its Clore Art Room. Her A–line shift dress, was in navy wool and trimmed with pastel pink French tweed, with the added touch of gold buttons. To the delight of the press, she posed for photos with cross-dressing artist Grayson Perry. He wore what he called his "ladies that lunch" black cocktail dress. "I thought it was appropriate for the occasion", said the artist.

The following day she wore a £50 brown silk jacquard dress, with an animal-print pattern, by the High Street label Hobbs when she visited foster carers in North London.

Using fashion to flatter has been a royal lady's trick of the trade for generations. Kate wore a suitably nautical boat print dress when she visited Portsmouth in February to see the progress of the new home of Ben Ainslie Racing. The black shift dress with a red and white boat print by Alice Temperley was from Somerset. She teamed it with an £810 cream wool Max Mara Studio Gilles coat, which served another royal fashion consideration, by enabling Kate to stand out in the crowd as she went on a brief walkabout outside the city's landmark Spinnaker Tower. As with so many of Kate's clothes both the coat and dress sold out the same day.

Despite being in her third trimester, Kate travelled further afield in the seventh and eighth months of her pregnancy with visits scheduled for Staffordshire and Kent. For her tour of the Emma Bridgewater pottery factory Kate wore a blue "Florrie" floral print dress by Seraphine, one she had worn before, under a matching blue wool coat by Sportmax. She also wore matching blue suede Jimmy Choo pumps and an L K Bennett Frome suede clutch bag in the exact matching shade. Then, and in the previous months, the Duchess proved that maternity wear can be flattering and fashionable was well as comfortable to wear.

THE ARRIVAL
OF PRINCE
GEORGE

The much-awaited royal baby was born at 4.24pm on Monday 22 July 2013. Catherine had very much wanted a natural birth and had opted to have her baby in the Lindo Wing of St Mary's Hospital, Paddington, just a five-minute car journey from the royal couple's temporary home at Nottingham Cottage in the grounds of Kensington Palace.

LEFT: *Hospital staff applaud as the new royal family happily greet the world outside the Lindo Wing of St Mary's Hospital, Paddington.*

The Lindo Wing has been a royal favourite since Princess Anne gave birth to her first child, Peter Phillips, there in November 1977. His sister Zara was born there four years later. Princess Diana gave birth to William at St Mary's in June 1982 and also to Harry in September 1984.

Media interest in the latest birth increased dramatically at the beginning of July, when parking bays for taxis and drop-off zones for visitors outside the Lindo Wing were suspended until the end of the month. Photographers and news crews began to mark out spaces for themselves on the opposite side of South Wharf Road, chaining stepladders together to reserve plots. By the end of the first week in July, barriers had been erected to form a series of press pens and the police were regularly monitoring the scene.

All that was needed was a sign that the baby was on its way. Catherine had told one well-wisher that it would be in mid-July. By the week beginning 15 July, it was reported that the mother-to-be was staying at Bucklebury with her parents and would be returning to London only on Friday 19 July. Carole Middleton was reported to have told friends the baby would be born under the Leo star sign, suggesting 23 July was the earliest it was due to arrive.

In the event it was the day before that things began to happen. Catherine went into labour in the early hours of the morning. A statement issued by her office at 7.30am announced that she had been admitted to St Mary's just before 6am, adding that "things are progressing as normal".

An eagle-eyed photographer noticed the royal car and a police back-up vehicle drive to the back of the Lindo Wing. Although he decided not to take a photograph and invade the privacy of a woman in labour, he tweeted a message announcing what he had seen and within an hour the hospital was deluged with photographers, reporters and camera crews.

ABOVE LEFT: *Marcus Setchell, surgeon and gynaecologist to the Queen during 1990–2008, has been brought back from retirement for special events such as the birth of Prince George.*

ABOVE: *Alan Farthing, one of the two surgeons who oversaw the birth. A consultant at St Mary's Hospital since 1997, he took over from Setchell as surgeon and gynaecologist to the Queen from 2008.*

RIGHT, TOP: *Jubilant but patient, patriotic crowds wait outside St Mary's Hospital for the royal couple to emerge with their little prince.*

RIGHT, BOTTOM: *On the evening of 22 July, a warm summer night, crowds celebrate and view the official birth notification outside Buckingham Palace.*

For the rest of the day there was very little to report because no details emerged from the hospital or the royal press teams until later. We knew that Catherine was staying in a suite of two rooms and that the cost of a one-night stay and delivery package was £6,265. We also knew that she was under the care of the Queen's current surgeon/gynaecologist Alan Farthing and his predecessor Marcus Setchell. During the day, which turned out to be one of the hottest of the year, crowds began to gather in the precincts of the hospital, sharing news with friends and relations on social networking sites.

Shortly after 8.30pm it was announced from Clarence House that a baby boy had been born at 4.24pm weighing 8lbs 6oz (3.79kg) and that mother and son were both doing well. Catherine had been in labour for about 11 hours, and the couple had chosen to have a few hours of privacy before sharing their news with the whole world, though William telephoned the Queen, his father and Prince Harry to tell them personally and both he and Catherine spoke to her parents to give them the good news.

An official announcement, signed by the doctors in attendance, was then driven from the Lindo Wing to Buckingham Palace where, following a long tradition, it was put on public display to the delight of the thousand or so members of the public gathered near to the railings. As he left the hospital, Marcus Setchell, who had delivered the infant, described him as a "wonderful, beautiful baby".

In a statement Prince Charles said he was "enormously proud and happy to be a grandfather for the first time", adding that it was "an incredibly special moment for William and Catherine".

In London the fountains of Trafalgar Square and Tower Bridge were both illuminated in blue, while at the top of the BT Tower the message "It's a Boy" shone across the night sky.

Prince William, who stayed at the hospital overnight, made a short statement: "We are both delighted." The Queen and Prince Philip announced that they were also "delighted". Prime Minister David Cameron said the birth was "an important moment in the life of our nation", while US President Barack Obama and wife Michelle sent their congratulations, adding, "We wish them all the happiness and blessings parenthood brings."

The next day more good wishes poured in. William's uncle Earl Spencer said, "We're all so pleased, it's excellent news." It was a poignant reminder that one person who would have loved this moment was the late Princess of Wales. Diana would have been 52 by now, and no doubt the world's most glamorous grandmother. The Earl continued: "My father always told us how Diana was born on such a blisteringly hot day, at Sandringham in 1961. It's another very happy summer's day, half a century on."

At 2pm the bells of Westminster Abbey rang for three hours to celebrate the birth, with 5,000 changes in a specially composed peal called Cambridge Surprise Royal. Across London, also at 2pm, a 41-gun salute was fired by the Royal Artillery Company in Green Park and a 62-gun salute was fired from Gun Wharf at the Tower of London.

Meanwhile it was announced that Adam Miell from Southampton was named as the first child born on the same day as the royal baby. He would receive a limited-edition commemorative silver coin.

Shortly after 3pm Catherine's hairdresser Amanda Tucker arrived at the hospital, followed a few minutes later by Catherine's parents. Smiling broadly, Michael and Carole later told reporters the baby is "absolutely beautiful", adding, "They're both doing really well, we're so thrilled."

Later in the afternoon, at 5.30pm, Prince Charles and the Duchess of Cornwall received huge cheers as they arrived at the Lindo Wing, both smiling happily and waving to well-wishers. The prince described his first grandson as "marvellous". Asked how the young prince was doing, he said, "You wait and see, you'll see in a minute."

Kensington Palace confirmed the Duchess would be discharged from St Mary's that evening and head for Kensington Palace. The statement added that

ABOVE: *"Her Royal Highness The Duchess of Cambridge was safely delivered of a son at 4.24pm today. Her Royal Highness and her child are both doing well." The official notice posted on an easel outside Buckingham Palace on the evening of the birth.*

the Cambridges "would like to reiterate their thanks to the hospital for the care and treatment they have all received".

Finally at 7.13pm the hundreds of assembled media and the crowd of several thousand well-wishers were rewarded with the moment they had been waiting for, some for quite a few days: William and Catherine emerged and descended the steps of the Lindo Wing to introduce their baby son to the world.

The prince held his son in his arms as he told reporters, "He has got a good pair of lungs on him, that's for sure. He is a big boy, he is quite heavy. We are still working on a name, and we'll have it as soon as we can."

The delighted couple revealed that William had been the first one to change a nappy. William joked that his son had more hair than he did and "thankfully"

LEFT: *The long-awaited arrival: William and Catherine emerge from St Mary's Hospital bearing their newborn son, to present him to the world for the first time.*

BELOW: *A tender moment as Catherine passes her precious bundle to William. The challenge never lets up for the Cambridges in balancing private intimacies with a life lived in public view, but they have become extremely skilled at this difficult art.*

PREVIOUS PAGES: *The massed ranks of press can be infinitely more daunting than the cheering public or sturdy police, but the Duke and Duchess face them for a brief chat with their usual charm, tolerance and good humour.*

LEFT: *Safe in his mother's arms, baby Prince George seemed half asleep. But his fingers were moving in what looked remarkably like his first royal wave.*

BELOW: *Prince William carries his son in a car seat to the back seat of the Range Rover. The car seat was carefully checked in the hospital – not only for the safety of the new heir to the throne but also because this special family is so much in the public eye and so very influential.*

his mother's looks. The Duchess said: "It's very emotional, it's such a special time, any parent will know what this feeling feels like."

The couple said they were looking forward to spending some time with their son at home, as Prince William said: "It's the first time we have seen him really, so we are having a proper chance to catch up."

They returned inside the hospital, emerging again soon afterwards with Prince William carrying his son in a car seat which he fitted into his Range Rover. The Duke drove while Catherine sat in the back proudly gazing at her new baby boy. With the crowds shouting and cheering, the royal parents waved as they left St Mary's Hospital heading for Kensington Palace.

The following day, the Queen visited them and the baby prince met his "thrilled" great-grandmother for the first time. After her departure, his name was announced, putting an end to public debate and betting: George Alexander Louis, to be known as Prince George of Cambridge.

George was, of course, the name chosen by the Queen's father on becoming king, George VI, and had been the bookies' favourite. Alexander was a name liked by Catherine, while Louis was thought to be in honour of Lord Louis Mountbatten, Prince Charles's beloved great-uncle on Prince Philip's side.

That same evening, the new family left London to spend some time with Catherine's family in Berkshire. There they would be able to enjoy privacy and wide family support as they began their cherished new life together.

LEFT: *Clearly emotional, exhausted, but very happy indeed, Catherine wore a blue polka-dot dress that echoed the dress worn by Princess Diana when she left hospital with the newborn William in 1982.*

WE FOUR

When George was born, Kate hoped to be able to look after her baby herself with occasional help from her mother Carole and a new housekeeper Antonella Fresolone. Italian-born Antonella was one of the three senior housemaids employed by the Queen, and was one of Her Majesty's most trusted members of staff. She worked at Buckingham Palace for 13 years and is popular with the other staff and her employer as well as being terrific at Italian cooking.

LEFT: *In this first official image of the royal family since the birth of their first baby, the Duke and Duchess of Cambridge pose with Prince George Alexander Louis of Cambridge, surrounded by Lupo, the couple's cocker spaniel, in the garden of the Middleton family home in August 2013.*

The Cambridges advertised for someone with "discretion, loyalty and reliability" and Antonella was expected, among other things, to care for the family's clothing, clean their home – including glassware and silverware – do the laundry and walk their black cocker spaniel Lupo. She also helped look after George.

With the three-week tour of New Zealand and Australia on the cards for the spring of 2014, however a full-time nanny was needed and Maria Borrallo was appointed. She will now have to divide her time between the new baby and the infant George, who like most two-year-olds will no doubt be a handful.

In another break with tradition, Catherine, like many first-time mums, has turned to her parents Carole and Michael for help in bringing up George. In previous generations, royal in-laws stayed firmly in the background. Diana's parents had very little to do with the upbringing of William and Harry. Her father, Earl Spencer, despite being a former equerry to the Queen, was never a personal guest of Her Majesty in his later life. The Middletons, by contrast, have frequently stayed on Prince Charles's Birkhall estate in Aberdeenshire and have twice been the Queen's guests in the Royal Ascot carriage procession.

During Catherine's first pregnancy, she and Carole were occasionally spotted shopping for clothes and nursery goods. In April 2013 they were seen picking up a £295 white wicker Moses basket from London's Blue Almonds store. Mother and daughter have ensured the nursery at Kensington Palace has a warm, personal touch to it, and did much of the decorating themselves. Catherine was seen looking at furniture at Kingcome Sofas in June of that year. According to the *Daily Express*, the Duke and Duchess of Cambridge will complete the nursery with a limited edition £399 Windsor Collection baby bath, which is a miniature version of a classic Victorian roll-top design.

In their engagement interview both William and Catherine praised the Middletons. The Duchess said of her parents, "They've been great over the years – helping me with difficult times. We see a lot of each other and they are very, very dear to me." William added, "Kate's got a very, very close family. I get on really well with them and I'm very lucky that they've been so supportive. Mike and Carole have been really loving and caring and really fun and have been really welcoming towards me so I've felt really a part of the family." They are so close that William opted to spend Christmas 2012 with the Middletons.

When Kate was suffering from morning sickness during her second pregnancy, Carole helped out again. She looked after Prince George, taking him in to local shops near to her £5 million mansion, Bucklebury Manor. One surprised assistant wrote on Twitter: "Served Kate Middleton's Mum and Prince George today at work. He is gorgeous!"

Carole also looked after the prince when William and Kate were in the USA. The doting grandmother took the 17-month-old to visit a farmer's market and let him sample the goods. He even went back to one stall for a second helping of Christmas pudding.

ABOVE: *Carole and Michael Middleton arrive at the Lindo Wing after the birth of Prince George. From the beginning the couple have been involved with the care and upbringing of their grandson, and Carole Middleton has been spotted out shopping for baby equipment in London.*

RIGHT: *Diana's love for William was never in doubt. This relaxed shot shows her playing with her seven-and-a-half-month old son at Kensington Palace, where William and Catherine are bringing up their new family.*

One significant change since the birth of George is that the Cambridges now have two dream homes. Apartment 1a Kensington Palace, the former home of Princess Margaret, has 20 rooms over four floors as well as a private walled garden and a small courtyard. It was renovated at the cost of £4.5million and will be the couple's official London residence.

In the next two years it is likely that they will spend most of their times at Anmer Hall, gifted to them by the Queen and just down the road from the monarch's Norfolk residence, Sandringham House. This will be a handy base for William who is currently working for the East Anglian Air Ambulance (EAAA) – as a pilot, though like Kate he will still be expected to carry out a number of official engagements on behalf of his grandmother.

With parents who enjoy everything from swimming to skiing, sport is likely to be a major part of their two children's lives. William also has fond memories of the treats organized by Diana, from trips to the cinema and McDonald's in Kensington to days out at theme parks such as Thorpe Park, where she made her sons queue up with other families rather than receive first-class treatment. Diana also encouraged her sons to consider the disadvantaged and took both William and Harry to hostels for the homeless run by Centrepoint; a charity the elder prince has been patron of since 2005. At the same time, both princes were taught by their parents to be mindful of their royal heritage and to bow when they meet the Queen and Prince Philip something they will make sure the new baby eventually learns.

Being a royal baby isn't all plain sailing. They must get used to the ever-present

ABOVE: *Kensington Palace was William's childhood home. He and Catherine took up residence here in 2013 following the refurbishment of Princess Margaret's apartment. "KP", as it is known in the family, has been a royal home since 1689.*

armed protection officers. Prince Harry in particular liked to give his the slip and once sneaked off into Kensington High Street, causing consternation back at the palace.

Another downside is the presence of the occasional members of the paparazzi. In Britain magazines and newspapers have generally been very good about not using snatched private photos of Prince George as his nanny walks him through Kensington Gardens. However, there is still a lucrative market overseas, especially in the USA, France, Germany and Italy, none of which have monarchies but which have always been fascinated by the House of Windsor and especially by Diana and Kate and their children.

BELOW: *A view of the Georgian country house Amner Hall on the Sandringham Estate at King's Lynn in Norfolk. This house was given to the Duke and Duchess as a wedding present by the Queen and will be their country residence.*

LEFT: *Prince Harry is seen chatting to members of the public as he leaves the Christmas Day service at Sandringham Church in 2014. Harry will be a key influence on his nephew's life and the bringing up of both royal siblings.*

RIGHT: *Pippa and James Middleton shown together at the Diamond Jubilee in 2012. All three siblings are very close and family time is of the utmost importance.*

At the beginning of October 2014 the Cambridges took legal action to warn off two photographers against trailing baby George, saying their behaviour amounted to "harassment". William in particular blames the press for causing the death of his mother in 1997. His spokesman said, "They want Prince George to lead as ordinary a life as possible as a child and he obviously can not do that if people are going to parks where children play and taking pictures of him."

With two royal children to protect the royal couple are likely to continue to fight to ensure their children don't have to go through the same harassment that William and Harry witnessed Diana suffering when they themselves were young.

Diana jokingly referred to Harry as "the back-up" and it is certainly vital for the royal dynasty to have more than one child in line to the throne since the eldest doesn't always become monarch. Both the Queen's father and grandfather were second sons. George V was set for a life in the navy until his elder brother Eddie died from influenza that developed into pneumonia in 1892. George VI became king in December 1936 after the abdication of his brother Edward VIII.

William has said he will be happy with two children, while Kate has reportedly told friends she would like three before she reaches the age of 35 in 2017. She is, of course, one of three siblings. She is just 20 months older than sister Pippa – there is a similar age gap between her own two – and less than five years older than brother James. They are incredibly close and meet up every few weeks or so, either in London or at the Middleton's house.

William knows from his own experience that a sibling is also a best friend. He and Harry have always been close and this bond was cemented after the death of Diana. William and Kate will hope that their new baby will be Prince George's greatest friend and supporter under the intense scrutiny that will face them both in the years and decades ahead.

RIGHT: *Prince Harry, the Duchess of Cambridge and Prince William visiting the poppy field art installation in the moat of the Tower of London, to commemorate the First World War. William and Harry' strong bond is bound to have a big affect on Prince George and his new sibling.*

PRINCE GEORGE'S CHRISTENING

The christening of new royal babies has tended to follow a traditional format, largely unchanged since the days of Queen Victoria. It includes two traditional items: a replica lace christening robe and the royal Lily Font.

LEFT: *Four generations of the Royal Family gather in The Morning Room at Clarence House in London for the official portrait for the christening of Prince George Alexander Louis of Cambridge.*

The ceremonies for the future Elizabeth II and princes Charles and William each lasted about 30 minutes and were conducted by the Archbishop of Canterbury, the senior cleric of the Church of England. Since Queen Victoria's time a hymn has been sung before the baby is placed into the arms of the main godparent, who in turn hands the infant to the Archbishop. After the service the royal family adjourn to another room to sign the baptismal register, before posing for photographs and cutting a christening cake.

A christening gown made for the baptism of Princess Victoria, the eldest child of Queen Victoria and Prince Albert, in February 1841 has been used at nearly every royal baptism for over 160 years. Like Victoria's wedding dress, it was made from Honiton lace over white satin.

In 1894 Queen Victoria gave the robe to the Duchess of York (later Queen Mary and grandmother to the present Queen). The future King Edward VIII and King George VI, their sister Princess Mary and three brothers were all baptized in it. In the next generation it was worn by the children of King George VI as well of those of Prince Henry, Duke of Gloucester, and of Prince George, Duke of Kent. The children of the Queen and of Princess Margaret were christened in it and it has subsequently been used for the christenings of seven of the Queen's grandchildren as well as other royal babies, including the grandchildren of Princess Margaret.

LEFT: *The only other time in British history when a member of the royal family lived to see the birth of a great-grandchild in direct line to the throne was in June 1894, when 75-year-old Queen Victoria welcomed the future King Edward VIII into the world. Here Victoria, dressed as always in deepest mourning, holds baby Edward, watched by Mary Duchess of York (later Queen Mary), standing on the left, and Alexandra Princess of Wales (later Queen Alexandra). The baby is wearing the beautiful Honiton lace christening robe.*

ABOVE: *A posed family shot after the christening of the future Elizabeth II on 29 May 1926. Back row left to right: the Duke of Connaught, King George V, the Duke of York and the Earl of Strathmore. Front row, left to right: Lady Elphinstone, Queen Mary, the Duchess of York holding Princess Elizabeth, the Countess of Strathmore and Princess Mary.*

The last baby to use the robe was Lady Louise Windsor, the daughter of Prince Edward, who was baptized on 24 April 2004 in the private chapel at Windsor Castle. By then, the satin was badly worn and the lace had turned from white to a creamy colour. The gown had already been mended in 1977 by the royal couturier Norman Hartnell for the christening of Princess Anne's son Peter Phillips on 22 December of that year. After Lady Louise's christening, the Queen commissioned a replica of the royal robe from her in-house design team, led by her senior dresser Angela Kelly.

Like the lace christening robe, the Lily Font was first used at the baptism of Queen Victoria's eldest child, Princess Victoria, in 1841. It was designed by Prince Albert and made by Barnard and Company on behalf of the London

ABOVE: *The christening of Prince Charles on 15 December 1948. Back row, left to right: Lady Patricia Brabourne, the Duke of Edinburgh, King George VI, the Hon David Bowes-Lyon, the Earl of Athlone (proxy for the King of Norway), Princess Margaret. Front row: Princess Elizabeth sits between Prince Philip's grandmother, the Dowager Marchioness of Milford Haven, on the left, and her own grandmother, Queen Mary.*

goldsmiths E & W Smith. The silver-gilt piece is 432 mm (17 inches) high and weighs 9.04 kg (319 oz). It was stored at Windsor Castle until the mid-1960s, when it was moved to the Tower of London to join other royal exhibits in the Jewel House.

In 1926 the future Elizabeth II was christened. The names of the new baby have traditionally been submitted by the parents to the monarch for approval. The Duke and Duchess of York (later King George VI and Queen Elizabeth) wanted to call their younger daughter Ann Margaret, but the king vetoed the idea and she was baptized Margaret Rose instead.

There were no problems with the names of the Yorks' eldest daughter, who was christened Elizabeth Alexandra Mary after her mother, her paternal great-grandmother Queen Alexandra (who had died the previous November) and paternal grandmother Queen Mary. In a letter to his son, King George V told the Yorks he approved of the name Elizabeth: "I like it & think it is a pretty name.' In a letter to his wife Queen Mary, George V wrote: "I have heard from Bertie about the names, he mentions Elizabeth, Alexandra, Mary. I quite approve & will tell him so, he says nothing about Victoria. I hardly think that necessary."

The ceremony was held on 29 May 1926 in the Private Chapel at Buckingham Palace, under the auspices of Cosmo Gordon Lang, Archbishop of York. The chapel was later completely destroyed when, in September 1940, it suffered a direct hit from a Luftwaffe bomb. Among the baby's godparents were Prince Arthur, Duke of Connaught, the third (and favourite) son of Queen Victoria. In an interesting link with the past, Arthur has been named after his godfather, the Duke of Wellington, the hero of Waterloo who shared the same birthday, 1 May.

Photos show the future Elizabeth II lying placidly in her mother's arms. During the service itself, however, she apparently cried so much that her nurse dosed her with dill water, an old-fashioned remedy, much to the amusement of her uncle, the Prince of Wales.

In December 1948, Charles, the first-born of Prince Philip and Princess Elizabeth, was baptized in the Music Room at Buckingham Palace. Geoffrey Fisher, Archbishop of Canterbury, conducted the ceremony on 15 December 1948 and the four-week-old future king was christened Charles Philip Arthur George. There are no limits to the number of royal names and all of Elizabeth's children were given four.

Prince William, like his father before him, was baptized in the Music Room at Buckingham Palace in 1982. The date chosen was 4 August, which was the Queen Mother's 82nd birthday, and the service was conducted by Robert Runcie, Archbishop of Canterbury. Unlike his father and grandmother, William was not baptized using consecrated Jordan water. *The Times* stated that ordinary water was used at the baptism, because the "Palace's supply of Jordan water [ran out] some royal babies ago".

ABOVE: *Princess Elizabeth holds her daughter Princess Anne on her christening at Buckingham Palace on 21 October 1950 with the Duke of Edinburgh at her side. Princess Anne is wearing the christening gown made from Honiton lace.*

AN EAGERLY AWAITED PORTRAIT: H.R.H. PRINCE CHARLES OF EDINBURGH IN THE ARMS OF HIS MOTHER, H.R.H. PRINCESS ELIZABETH, DUCHESS OF EDINBURGH, AFTER HIS CHRISTENING ON DECEMBER 15.

The first portraits of H.R.H. Prince Charles of Edinburgh, infant son of T.R.H. Princess Elizabeth and the Duke of Edinburgh, who was born on Sunday, November 14, have been eagerly awaited by the whole country, the Commonwealth and foreign nations. The baby Prince was photographed after his christening at Buckingham Palace on December 15. This camera study shows him in the arms of his mother after the ceremony. It took place at 3.30 p.m. in the White and | Gold Music Room of the Palace. The Archbishop of Canterbury officiated, assisted by the Rev. M. F. Foxell, precentor and Sub-Dean of his Majesty's Chapels Royal and Domestic Chaplain to the King. The infant received the names of Charles Philip Arthur George, and the service was attended by their Majesties, members of the Royal family and a few close friends. Other photographs taken on the occasion appear elsewhere in this issue.

LEFT: *The proud mother. Princess Elizabeth was only 22 when she gave birth to Prince Charles. "Don't you think he is quite adorable?" she asked a friend. "I still can't believe he is really mine." The baby wore the traditional royal christening gown made for Queen Victoria's eldest daughter, Victoria.*

RIGHT: *Charles and Diana look lovingly at their first-born son during his christening on 4 August 1982. Charles wrote to his godmother Lady Brabourne: "The arrival of our small son has been an astonishing experience and one that has meant more to me than I could ever have imagined."*

The baby's six godparents included Constantine II, King of the Hellenes (his father's second cousin); Lady Susan Hussey, one of the Queen's ladies-in-waiting, whose husband Marmaduke was at one time Chairman of the BBC; and Sir Laurens van der Post, the South African writer and explorer.

Prince William's christening cake was, like his father's had been, the top layer of his parents' wedding cake – a tradition the royals like to observe. According to coverage in *The Times*, in a touching gesture, pieces of the cake were "distributed to 182 men of the Welsh Guards and the Parachute Regiment wounded in the Falklands conflict". This was a reminder that the future William V had been born just a week after the Argentine surrender on 14 June 1982.

Prince George was baptized at the Chapel Royal, at St James's Palace. The Chapel Royal was the setting for the wedding of Queen Victoria and Prince Albert in 1840 and of the present Queen's grandparents, the future George V and Queen Mary in 1893. It was also where Princess Beatrice was baptized in 1988. Most significantly for William, it was where his mother's body lay in the days after her death in August 1997. William and Harry came there to see Diana's remains on the eve of her funeral, the coffin was lowered so that they could see over it, and the princes have never forgotten the peace and beauty of the chapel, as they said their final private goodbye before accompanying the coffin on its very public journey to Kensington Palace.

The date of George's christening had been chosen to fit in with the schedule of the Queen and Prince Philip, who normally spend August and September at Balmoral Castle in Aberdeenshire. In June the Duke of Edinburgh had spent 11 days in the London Clinic for an exploratory operation on his abdomen and had spent the summer months recuperating.

As the day grew nearer there was speculation in the media about the choice of godparents. The actual list of seven names was kept secret until the day.

As with William's own christening in 1982, there was surprise at the lack of royal names on the list. William's only royal godparent was Princess Alexandra, first cousin to the Queen and a close friend of Prince Charles.

William and Kate had only one relation on their team as well: the Princess Royal's daughter, Zara Tindall, a year older than William and part of the close circle who helped the prince and his brother in the dark days following their mother's death.

None of Diana's side of the family was asked to be a godparent, but Julia Samuel, a close friend of the late princess, was chosen as a godmother. Her sister Sabrina has been a girlfriend of Prince Charles. Julia set up Child Bereavement UK, a charity that helps supports families who lose one or more children. Diana was there for the launch and today William is one of the charity's patrons.

The third godmother is Emilia Jardine-Paterson, who has known Kate since they both attended Marlborough College. The two women have remained close and holidayed together in Ibiza in 2007 when William and Kate temporarily split.

The four godfathers include William van Cutsem, the youngest of Hugh and Emilie van Cutsem's four sons. Hugh, who was a close friend of Prince Charles, died the month before the christening and the prince and his two sons attended his funeral.

Oliver Baker, who shared a house with both William and Kate at St Andrews when they were all students, and also the rural farmhouse they lived in during their final year, was an obvious choice as another godfather.

The youngest godfather is Hugh, Earl Grosvenor, the heir to the fabulously wealthy Duke of Westminster, who owns 100 acres of real estate in Mayfair and 200 acres of Belgravia. Hugh's sister Lady Tamara married William van

ABOVE: *Wearing a sky-blue Steward Parvin coat and hat, the Queen leaves the Chapel Royal, where her three-month-old great grandson has just been christened. She is followed by the Duchess of Cornwall.*

RIGHT: *A well-behaved Prince George arrives with his father Prince William for his christening. According to the guests, he smiled throughout the private ceremony.*

Cutsem's brother Ed in 2004 at Chester Cathedral at a service attended by William and Harry as well as the Queen and Prince Philip.

Finally Jamie Lowther-Pinkerton, a former SAS Major, who was private secretary to both William and Harry from 2005 until a few weeks before the christening, was also asked to be a godfather. His son William was a pageboy at the royal wedding in 2011.

For his baptism Prince George wore the replica of the Honiton lace, silk-lined christening robe made for Queen Victoria's first child, Princess Victoria. The silver gilt Lily Font designed by Prince Albert in 1841, was brought to the Chapel Royal from the Tower of London.

Prince George behaved well throughout the service and the ensuing photo session. One guest said later: "He went in smiling, came out smiling and, as far as we aware smiled throughout." It hadn't been all plain sailing as Prince William pointed out when he joked, "It's the first time he's been quiet all day."

Both Prince Harry and Pippa Middleton read passages from the gospels and the congregation sang the hymns 'Breathe on Me, Breath of God' and 'Be Thou My Vision', and one of the two anthems chosen was 'Blessed Jesu. Here we stand.' The latter was composed for Prince William's christening.

The Archbishop of Canterbury, Justin Welby, baptized the infant prince, making the sign of the cross with Jordan water, another royal tradition.

The royal party then made its way to Clarence House, which adjoins St James's Palace, for a tea party and a slice of William and Kate's wedding cake, made by Fiona Cairns, a tier of which had been saved for this hoped-for event.

Then the guests posed for a series of photographs including one featuring four generations: the Queen, Charles, William and George. It is the first time a monarch has posed with three direct heirs to the throne since Queen Victoria attended the christening of the future Edward VIII in 1894.

At a fund-raising reception at Kensington Palace, just a few hours after the baptism, Kate told guests: "It went very well. It was very emotional and a lovely day."

ABOVE: *Royalist Terry Hutt poses outside St James' Palace ahead of the christening of Prince George. This low-key event was watched by fans and well-wishers, some of whom camped out the night before.*

LEFT: *Catherine holds her son following his christening at Chapel Royal in St James' Palace in central London on 23 October, 2013. Prince George is wearing a replica of the gown made for the baptism of Princess Victoria in 1841.*

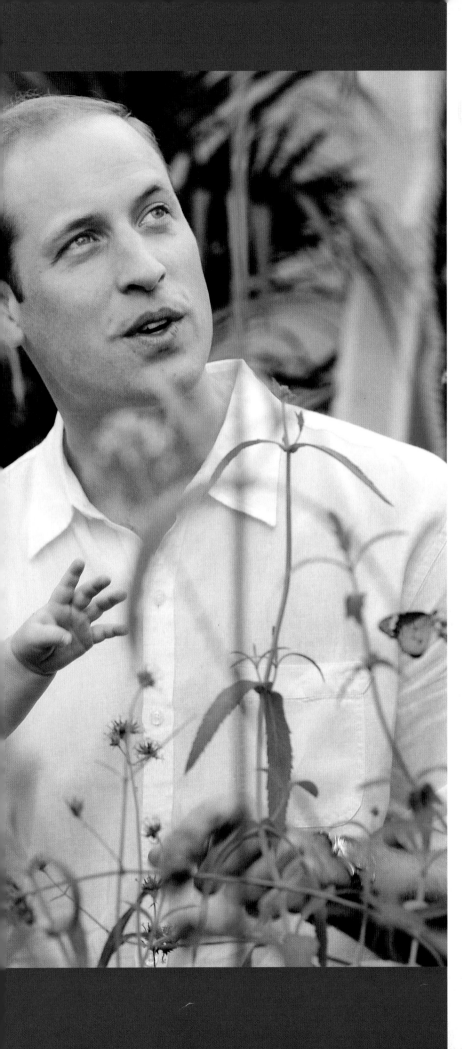

ROYAL GEORGE

After the massive news coverage of his christening, Prince George spent the rest of the year away from photographers and royal fans at Kensington Palace, with occasional breaks with the Middletons at Bucklebury. Although he was shielded from prying eyes, occasional snippets of nursery gossip were leaked by his proud parents whenever well-wishers or hopeful journalists asked them about the young prince.

LEFT: *This photograph was taken on 2 July 2014, to mark Prince George's first birthday. The royal couple and their son were visting the butterflies exhibition at the Natural History Museum in London.*

203

A few days after the christening, William spoke of his desire to take his son to see his own favourite football team, Aston Villa. In an interview to mark the 150th anniversary of the formation of the Football Association, William was asked if his son would follow the same club. A smiling Duke said: "When Villa thrash Man U at Villa Park my son will be there." Just why William has supported the Birmingham-based club since his early teens has never been explained; nor why he wants to see them "thrash" Manchester United!

There was more parental pride later in the year when the Queen and three future kings gathered together at Sandringham to celebrate Christmas. A record crowd, boosted by false rumours that George would be making an appearance at the traditional church service on the estate, had to make do with nearly 30 other royals, including William, Kate and a bearded Harry. After church the Cambridges helped to collect flowers from the well-wishers and when asked, "Where's the baby?", Kate replied "He's having a lovely day but is more interested in the wrapping paper than the presents." William added: "We've had a good morning with George and I can't wait until next year when's he bigger."

Later in the day, the Queen mentioned her first great grandson in her annual Christmas broadcast. The proud monarch said, "Here at home my family is a little larger this year," adding that the birth of a baby helps people to think about the future with "renewed happiness and hope. For the parents life will never be quite the same again." She went on to speak about George's christening, while previously unseen film footage was played. At one point Kate was heard trying to encourage her son to look at the official photographer Jason Bell, saying "Good boy, George." According to the Queen, "It was a happy occasion, bringing together four generations."

It was photographs of a completely different kind that brought George's next public appearance to the world's attention. Paparazzi photos of Kate carrying George as she descended aircraft steps en route to a Middleton family holiday on the island of Mustique, appeared in a UK celebrity magazine in February 2014. The Cambridges zealously protect their privacy and William has held the paparazzi in contempt since the involvement of freelance photographers in causing the car crash that killed his mother. So when they didn't complain after the clearly private holiday snaps were published, many royal commentators were taken by surprise.

Kate once sued a photographer for taking snaps of her playing tennis the Christmas before her marriage. She also complained about press harassment when she was briefly working in London and was photographed on a coffee break.

Some legal experts pointed out the couple were sending mixed messages about what they considered on and off limits, and could be accused of exercising image control rather than protecting their right to privacy. In this case the photos were published after the magazine checked with Kensington Palace and was told that the Duchess would be unlikely to complain about them.

RIGHT: *The Duke and Duchess of Cambridge arriving for the Christmas Day service at Sandringham. Prince George was at home unwrapping presents. Later that day the Queen mentioned her first great grandson in her annual broadcast.*

The photos showed Kate as a very hands-on mother, something she had hoped to be throughout George's childhood. Initially it was suggested that the Duchess would not be hiring help to look after her son, but when he was seven months old she had a change of heart and, with a forthcoming tour of Australasia on the cards, it was imperative to employ a nanny to look after the prince while his parents were carrying out public engagements.

The Cambridges had so far relied on Carole Middleton as well as the Duke's former nanny Jessie Webb to help look after their son. Now they turned to Spanish-born Maria Teresa Turrion Borrallo, who was one of the names on a shortlist sent to them by the prestigious Norland College, which has been training nannies since it was founded in 1892. Maria, who was appointed to the full-time position and would live in, had the opportunity to get to know George's routine and habits while William and Kate enjoyed a week-long break in the Maldives in early March. Sadly for them, they missed George's first crawl, which happened at Kensington Palace while they were away. By 17 March, when Kate was presenting shamrocks to the Irish Guards regiment at Aldershot, he was, according to his mother, "crawling and eating" a lot.

The private holiday enabled the Duke and Duchess to rest before they undertook a hectic tour of New Zealand and Australia. Both Commonwealth countries eagerly awaited the visit since not only because Kate was making her debut in the Southern Hemisphere but also because it was announced that Prince George was also joining them. It was a case of history repeating itself since William, aged nine months, accompanied Charles and Diana on their 1983 visit to both countries.

A photograph of the three Cambridges and their dog Lupo was released ahead of the tour. Taken by Jason Bell, who had taken the official christening photos, these showed the family posing at an open window in their Kensington Palace apartment with George clearly intrigued by the family pet.

The royal party arrived in Wellington, New Zealand, on Monday, 7 April, at the start of the three-week tour. William and Kate would carry out 48 engagements and George, it was hoped, would also be making several appearances.

Kensington Palace would not specify which engagements George might appear at. William had memorably had his first "crawlabout" on the lawns of Government House in New Zealand and it was anticipated that the George might do the same. He was also going to be based there for some of the visit, mainly in the care of nanny Maria.

The first glimpse of the prince was, in fact, at Sydney airport where the royal party was changing flights. Kate carried George, who was wearing a navy blue buttoned-up shirt and matching trousers.

LEFT: *William and Catherine arrive in Wellington in April 2014, at the beginning of their three-week tour of Australia and New Zealand. This was Prince George's first official trip overseas.*

By the time they arrived in Wellington, he was wearing a white shirt and shorts with a beige jumper and shoes. Although the arrival was a blustery one, it was summer down under and so Kate had bought him a selection of clothes suitable for a hot climate. She was spotted shopping at Baby Gap in Kensington a few days before they set off.

George's first royal engagement in a lifetime of duty occurred at Government House two days after the Cambridges arrived there. It wasn't a posed shot in the gardens as it had been in 1983 but a more entertaining one inside. The royal prince joined ten other babies at a playgroup organized by the Plunket Society which provides free parental support services to more than nine out of ten New Zealand babies.

Dressed in navy blue "sailboat smocked dungarees" by the British designer Rachel Riley, George was in fine form as Kate carried him on her hip. He playfully chewed her hair and stared with interest at the other babies. Despite being an only child at the time, he had no problem crawling towards the others and stealing their toys, watched by his parents as they chatted to other parents, including a gay couple. Kate occasionally wiped some dribble from his mouth, making sure he looked his best for the photos that would be syndicated across the world in a matter of hours.

In 1983 has been Diana who stole the limelight. In 2014 it was über-cute George whom everyone was talking about and he was soon dubbed "the Republican slayer" thanks to the very positive press coverage.

At a reception a few days later, William told guests that he thought his son would grow up to be a prop forward, something guaranteed to delight the rugby-loving Kiwis. The prince also revealed his son didn't sleep through the night until he was five months old.

On their final day in New Zealand, Kate had to apologize to the crowds during a walkabout as well-wishers were hoping to see the prince in the flesh. She said that her "very podgy baby" was with his nanny and fast asleep.

The prince was wide awake when the royal party arrived in Sydney on 16 April. In a speech to VIPs at Sydney Opera House, William said: "George is now busy forging his own link with Australia." He added: "Catherine and I were very grateful for the many kind messages and gifts from across the country that we received when George was born." The Duke went on to say, "I suspect George's first word might be 'bilby' – only because 'koala' is harder to say. We really look forward to our time here together as a family."

Later it was neither animal that George got to know, but instead a massive cuddly wombat, which was presented to him by the Governor-General, Sir Peter Cosgrove.

The baby prince did get to see a bilby – a type of rabbit-like marsupial – when he visited Sydney's Taronga Zoo to meet one that was to be named after him. He squealed with delight when he saw the real-life creature and attempted to reach down and grab its ears until his father pulled him back.

RIGHT: *Prince George plays with toys during a visit to the Plunket nurse and parents group at Government House in Wellington. Plunket is a national not-for-profit organization that provides care for children and families in New Zealand.*

FOLLOWING PAGES: *Having completed their tour of New Zealand, William, Catherine and George arrive in Sydney on 16 April 2014. The Duchess wore a bright yellow dress by Roksanda Ilincic.*

To the delight of the crowd and the gathered photographers, George proved a star turn at the zoo, waving his arms and legs around in delight at all he saw. Well nearly all he saw. When he was handed a stuffed toy bilby, he threw it to the floor in disgust – much to his parents' embarrassment. "He loves it really!" said William as Kate bent down to retrieve it.

At a children's tea party near to Uluru, or Ayers Rock as it used to be called, Kate revealed that George had "grown an extra fat roll" during the tour and that "he's been changing so much while we've been away."

He was to change even more when he returned home. In June he was photographed walking, albeit a bit unsteadily, as Kate lightly held on to his hands. The prince was at Cirencester Park Polo Club in Gloucestershire, where William was playing in a charity polo match on Father's Day.

A month later George celebrated his first birthday with a party at Kensington Palace attended by his great-grandmother, the Queen, who stayed for 50 minutes and chatted to the Middleton family and the prince's godparents.

There was more celebration in December when Kate took him to two Christmas-themed events. The first was the Winter Wonderland in Hyde Park, where the prince, dressed in white, enjoyed a session on the teapot ride. Then on the weekend before Christmas his parents took him to another winter wonderland, this time in Thursford, Norfolk, following their arrival at Anmer Hall. George met Father Christmas on Santa's Magical Journey and he was given a wooden train set.

It was made clear that George wouldn't be seen in public over the Christmas holidays. For this reason, as well as to thank the press for not publishing paparazzi snaps of him in the London parks, the couple released three charming shots of the 16-month-old prince sitting on some steps at Kensington Palace looking very mischievous. It was a perfect end to George's first full year.

IT'S A GIRL!

Her Royal Highness Princess Charlotte of Cambridge was born at 8.34am on Saturday 2 May 2015, weighing a very healthy 8lb 3oz (3.71kg). Although somewhat overdue, the new princess eventually made a speedy entry into the world, arriving just two-and-a-half hours after the Duchess of Cambridge was admitted to the hospital.

LEFT: *The Duchess of Cambridge waves at the assembled crowds as the happy parents present their daughter to the world, a mere ten hours after her birth.*

It was called "The Second Great Kate Wait" since, as with Prince George, the latest royal baby was in no hurry to appear.

William and Kate kept their due date to themselves, though on 18 March, on a visit to a children's centre, the Duchess told a volunteer she was expecting "mid to late April. Not long to go now!" Westminster City Council seemed to have taken the soon-to-be mother at her word and suspended parking areas outside the Lindo Wing of St Mary's Hospital, from 15–30 April.

Royal watchers had begun to arrive and camp out from the 15th, but what was different this time is that the Kensington Palace press team was determined not to have the vast unmanageable press contingent that blocked the hospital grounds for weeks last time. Press places were allocated weeks before the birth and the photographers and news teams were told the press area would only become operational once the Duchess had been admitted.

Meanwhile Kate spent the last week or so keeping resolutely with child. A couple of days before what was reported to be her due date of 25 April she was at Bucklebury Farm Park, petting the animals with young George. She was also spotted in Zara Home near to "KP" where she bought a doormat, towels, padded blue gingham coat hangers and a picnic set. Asked by an eager reporter why the items were all coloured blue an assistant flatly replied "I guess it's her favourite colour".

Kate was also seen driving out of Buckingham Palace twice the week before the birth. It was believed she had been taking George to use the royal swimming pool.

In a thoughtful gesture the Cambridges sent coffee and pastries to the growing army of fans who had established a mini-camp outside the Lindo. The pink ribbon around the boxes of cakes caused much chatter from the loyalists who were all keeping their fingers crossed for a baby princess.

ABOVE: *The royal couple thanked ardent fans for their patience in awaiting the arrival of their second child by sending boxes of pastries and coffee on the morning of Tuesday 28 April 2015.*

OPPOSITE, TOP: *Tony Appleton, a town crier, once again chose to celebrate the new royal arrival by ringing out the news in front of the crowds of well-wishers and press from around the world.*

The royal couple also sent a cake and a card to one of the first to arrive, Terry Hutt, who turned 80, and which sent him "over the moon".

Finally the news everyone had been waiting for came in a tweet from Kensington Palace, around 6.30am on Saturday 2 May. "HRH The Duchess of Cambridge was admitted to St Mary's Hospital, Paddington, London and is in the early stages of labour." A second tweet added that the Duchess had travelled by car and that the Duke was with her.

More tweets were sent to all the accredited media and within a couple of hours the street outside the private maternity unit was crammed with news teams from the UK, USA, Canada, France, Germany, Australia and New Zealand.

Inside the Lindo, the birth of the baby was being overseen by Guy Thorpe-Beeston, Surgeon Gynaecologist to the Royal Household, who is one of the country's leading obstetricians. Assisting him was Alan Farthing, the Queen's Surgeon Gynaecologist, who has worked for the Queen's medical household since 2008, and was present at the birth of Prince George.

With the timing of Kate's arrival at hospital being similar to July 2013 when she gave birth to George, press and people were preparing for a lengthy wait, with the possibility of a 4.30pm birth like last time or even later. Thus few could have predicted that at 11.11am Kensington Palace would announce "HRH The Duchess of Cambridge was safely delivered of a daughter at 8.34am. The baby weighs 8lb 3oz. The Duke of Cambridge was present for the birth." The statement added "HRH and her child are both doing well."

As with the birth of George, there was a delay announcing the news to the world so that William could let his parents, grandparents and the Middleton family know of the arrival. Prince Harry who was in Australia at the time was also contacted.

The Queen, we were told, was "delighted with the news" that her fifth great grandchild had arrived and she used sartorial elegance to show she was thrilled it

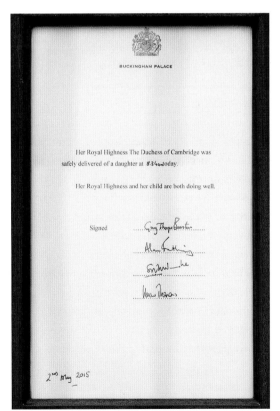

ABOVE: *An easel with the official announcement was placed within the grounds of Buckingham Palace shortly after news of the birth was announced on twitter. In place for just 24 hours, thousands of people arrived to view it.*

217

was a girl. Arriving in Richmond, North Yorkshire, to attend a military parade the Queen was positively beaming in a rose pink wool coat, designed by Karl Ludwig, and a matching hat designed by her senior dresser Angela Kelly.

Meanwhile back at St Mary's Hospital, Kate's hairdresser Amanda Cook Tucker was reportedly spotted entering the Lindo Wing which suggested that the Duchess might be released the same day. William's cousin, Zara Tindall, had left hospital five hours after giving birth to daughter Mia, but no other senior royal lady had ever left on the same day she'd had a baby.

The fact that no family members had arrived to visit also suggested the Cambridges might leave on Saturday afternoon. Prince Charles and the Duchess of Cornwall did however release a statement that they were "absolutely delighted" with the arrival of the new princess. Earlier in the week Charles had said he was hoping for a granddaughter. Earl Spencer, Prince William's uncle, said: "It's wonderful news – we are all thrilled for the four of them."

Shortly before 4pm, William emerged from the main entrance to the Lindo Wing, and prepared to drive to Kensington Palace. He told reporters "we're very, very happy," adding: "I'm just going home to pick up George."

Twenty minutes later there was a huge roar from the crowd as Prince George arrived with his father. The tiny prince started to toddle down the pavement but overwhelmed by the mass of cameras opposite, he clung to his father's leg. William picked him up and, urging him to wave, rewarded him with a kiss for his efforts.

ABOVE: *Prince William left Catherine's side briefly to collect Prince George and bring him to visit his new baby sister.*

OPPOSITE: *The Duke and Duchess of Cambridge look up to see hospital staff at the windows of another St Mary's building opposite.*

OPPOSITE: *William and Catherine gaze adoringly at their newborn daughter, whom they named after her grandfather Prince Charles, her grandmother Princess Diana, and her great grandmother, the Queen. Charlotte is also her aunt, Pippa Middleton's middle name.*

BELOW: *William and Catherine proudly introduce their newborn daughter to the world for the first time.*

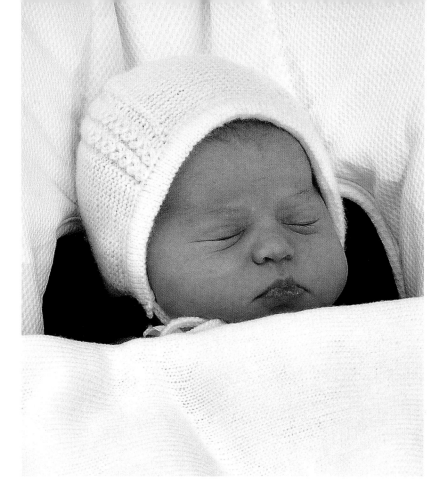

OPPOSITE: *The Duke of Cambridge carries his daughter to their waiting Range Rover as the royal couple prepare to depart for Kensington Palace with the newest member of their family.*

LEFT: *A sleeping Princess Charlotte leaves for home. Born just 10 hours earlier, the new princess appeared to sleep through her first public engagement.*

Later it emerged that George had left by the back entrance to the Lindo Wing, as William was concerned to protect his son from too much public scrutiny. It was after all only the first time since his birth that George had been seen out and about on an official appearance in the UK since he too left the hospital following his birth.

News spread around the waiting crowd that William and Kate were due to leave the hospital later in the day. At 6.12pm there was another roar as the couple appeared at the main entrance to the hospital. Kate was carrying the baby princess who was fast asleep and oblivious to all the attention she was getting.

The baby wore a knitted cream hat and a shawl designed by G H Hurt & Son Ltd, which has a longstanding connection with the royal household. Kate looked remarkably well and relaxed despite giving birth just ten hours earlier. Stylish as ever, she wore a Jenny Packham shift dress with a delicate buttercup print, as well as her trademark nude high heels.

The royal couple waved to both sides of the street as well as to hospital staff gathered in the windows of the Queen Elizabeth the Queen Mother Wing. They then returned inside for a few minutes to thank the maternity staff and to strap their new baby into her car seat.

In a repetition of the birth of George, William carried his daughter down to his Range Rover and fastened the seat into the car as Kate settled herself in the back seat. The prince then climbed into the driver's seat.

Waving to the crowds of royal fans, the royal couple drove off at a stately pace through the hospital grounds, heading for Kensington Palace and their new life together as a family of four.

CREDITS

The publishers would like to thank the following sources for their kind permission to reproduce the pictures in this book.

Key: l=Left, r=Right.

All Photography courtesy of Getty Images, except for the following:

Corbis:
190-1 (Jason Bell/epa)

Press Association Images:
170r (Michael Stephens/PA Archive)

Mary Evans Picture Library:
196 (Illustrated London News Ltd)

Rex Features:
23; 46 (Matt Phelvin); 56-7 (Susannah Ireland); 60-1 (David Hartley); 64 (Anthony Upton); 146 (Tim Rooker); 147 (Action Press); 170l (Nils Jorgensen);

Every effort has been made to acknowledge correctly and contact the source and/or copyright holder of each picture and Carlton Books Limited apologises for any unintentional errors or omissions, which will be, corrected in future editions of this book.